SCIENCE
COMES CLOSER TO
THE BIBLE
ON THE HISTORY OF THE EARTH

ARIMASA KUBO

Science Writer

SCIENCE
COMES CLOSER TO
THE BIBLE
ON THE HISTORY OF THE EARTH

What is Scientific Creationism?

Translated by Iwao Miyamoto and Miriam Doi
EastWest United Corporation

ACW Press
Phoenix, Arizona 85013

Science Comes Closer to the Bible
Copyright ©2001 Arimasa Kubo
All rights reserved

Cover Design by Eric Walljasper Design
Interior design by Pine Hill Graphics

Packaged by ACW Press
5501 N. 7th Ave., #502
Phoenix, Arizona 85013
www.acwpress.com
The views expressed or implied in this work do not necessarily reflect those of ACW Press. Ultimate design, content, and editorial accuracy of this work is the responsibility of the author(s).

Publisher's Cataloging-in-Publication
(Provided by Quality Books, Inc.)

Kubo, Arimasa.
    Science comes closer to the bible : (on the history
of the Earth) : what is scientific creationism? /
Arimasa Kubo ; translated by Iwao Miyamoto and Miriam
Doi. -- 1st ed., English ed.
    p. cm.
    Includes bibliographical references.
    ISBN: 1-892525-51-8

    1. Creationism. 2. Bible and science. 3. Bible.
O.T. Genesis--Criticism, interpretation, etc.
I. Title.

BS651.K83 2001   231.7'652
                           QBI01-200330

Printed in the United States of America.

Contents

✦

CHAPTER THREE

Sudden Enviromental Change
Due to the Great Flood 83

CHAPTER FOUR

The Age of Man and Planet Earth 139

Quotations with [*] mark are translated from Japanese.

About the Author

✦

ARIMASA KUBO was born in Hyogo Prefecture, Japan, in 1955. He graduated from the Tokyo Bible Seminary in 1982. Today, he is the chief writer for an evangelistic magazine *Remnant*, and representative of Remnant Publishing. He is also involved in a wide range of projects to promote understanding of the Bible.

He is author of a number of books in Japanese, including *The World of Scientific Creationism*, *A Sealed Ancient History of Japan and Israel 2—Buddhism & Nestorian Christianity Edition* (both published by Tokuma-shoten, a major publisher in Japan), *The Coming History*, *Life Beyond the Grave*, *Buddha and the Christian God*, *Events in the Last Days*, and *Israelites Came to Ancient Japan*.

His books have been translated into English, Korean, and Taiwanese, and are widely read.

About this Book

✦

THIS BOOK is a compilation of my articles about the origin of the earth and of life which appeared in the Japanese language magazine *Remnant*.

As the articles were being published, the flood of letters and telephone calls to the magazine made me realize that a lot of people had become interested in scientific creationism (creation science).

Today, the scientific explanation for the origin of the atmosphere, the oceans, the land, and of the earth itself has been vastly revised. And with every change, science comes closer to what the Bible has been saying all along.

The purpose of this book is to introduce recent scientific theories, and show how they are coming closer to the Bible. I sincerely hope this book will help you become more familiar with scientific creationism, and that it will deepen your understanding of what the Bible really is.

Arimasa Kubo

November 1, 2001

FOREWORD

by Masami Usami

I AM HAPPY to write the foreword to the English edition of *Science Comes Closer to the Bible*. It deals with creation science in a broad and simple manner so that a complete novice can easily read it. It also includes wonderful information which will serve well as a science primer.

As the title of this book indicates, the explanations of science certainly are coming closer to the Bible. Of course there is no cause to believe the present consensus of scientists is correct. Because of the possibility that changes will occur in theories based on science, which are not in agreement with the Biblical Record, we must be cautious about forming conclusions.

In chapters one and two, the author presents his understanding of the variations in modern science and the history of the earth. Everyone concerned with science and the history of the earth needs to consider this presentation.

The writer, in chapter three, "Sudden Environmental Change Due To The Great Flood," deals with the problems of physical geography, meteorology, longevity of life and many suggestions which are intertwined with these problems. Furthermore, it shows that a great flood actually happened, as recorded in the Bible, introducing many interesting evidences. It is not written in technical jargon, but in easily understandable language, which we can discern at once.

Chapter four, "The Age of Man and Planet Earth," deals with the age of the earth and man from the standpoint of creation, and clearly shows the evolutionist position to be in error. First, using the most widely trusted method for carbon 14 dating, that developed by Libby, scientists have tested human bones for their ages. The author introduced data showing that, according to these tests, the oldest bones are estimated at only 20,000 to 40,000 years. He also gives scientific evidence that shows that the long ages claimed by evolution do not agree with the physical facts on the earth.

It is possible for changes to occur in science, so the writer's understanding cannot be considered complete. We must be extremely cautious to determine whether or not ideas truly agree with the Bible. However, this book brings enlightenment to us on many matters relating to scientific creation. We may well think of this book as a challenge to modern thinking, as to whether or not modern ideas are good.

It is my hope that the English edition will also be widely read.

Masami Usami, M.D.
President, Creation Science Association of Japan
Director, Ibarakimachi Municipal Hospital

INTRODUCTION

✦

A Message To English Speakers
by Arimasa Kubo (author) and Iwao Miyamoto (translator)

ON THE OCCASION of publication of the English language version of *Science Comes Closer to the Bible*, we would like to offer a few remarks.

> "...And how can they hear without someone preaching to them? And how can they preach unless they are sent?" (Rom. 10:14,15).

Historically speaking, our country of Japan has been the land most distant from the Good News. But we are deeply grateful that even to us, the people of this country at the end of the earth, the message of both the Old and New Testaments has been proclaimed and the promise of God, creator of the heavens and the earth, "...that you may bring my salvation to the ends of the earth..." (Isaiah 49:6, Acts 13:47) has been fulfilled.

The spread of the Gospel to this country of Japan has been largely due to the efforts in recent times of people from English-speaking countries. It was not until the revocation of the Tokugawa government policies, which were enforced during the three hundred years of the feudal Edo Period to outlaw Christianity, that freedom of religious expression was finally recognized.

With the establishment of the Meiji government in 1868 and its efforts to extend a hand of friendship to Western nations, God called many Christian believers from mainly English-speaking countries (including ministers of the Church as well as common followers of Christ) and filled them with missionary zeal to bring the Gospel to this country at the end of the earth.

One example of these servants of God was an American who became popularly known as Professor William Smith Clark and won the affection and respect of all Japanese, Christian or otherwise. Professor Clark, although little known in present-day America, was the founder of Massachusetts Agricultural College and an outstanding commander (General) in the U.S. Civil War.

He came to Japan in 1887 at the invitation of Japan's then Meiji government and was appointed as Head of Staff (vice-principal) and Professor of Agriculture, Science, Mathematics and English at the Sapporo School of Agriculture (the predecessor to the modern-day Hokkaido National University) which was opened in Hokkaido, the northernmost island of the four major islands in the Japanese archipelago.

Professor Clark's stay in Japan was just eight short months but his contribution during that time to Japan's modernization was enormous. Of all the many facets of this contribution to Japan, one which deserves special mention is the support he gave to Japan's "spiritual" modernization. In other words, although only a common Christian believer, he presented Christianity, the Good News, to his students with passionate enthusiasm.

From among those whom he taught, many future leaders of Japan's Christian church were later raised up and the first independent church to be built by Japanese (the Sapporo Independent Church of Christ) was realized.

At the time of his departure from Japan, Professor Clark is well-known by every Japanese for his parting words, "Boys be ambitious!" It is said that he also added the words "in Christ."

The enormous achievements of Professor William Smith Clark were of course built on the foundations which were laid before him by a great many other English speakers who were filled with the earnest desire to bring the Word of God to Japan. Professor Clark's example is given to illustrate the extent to which we Japanese owe a debt of gratitude to the people of English-speaking lands.

It is estimated that Christians in Japan today comprise just 1 percent of Japan's total population, a statistic which has long remained constant. In this regard, we are reminded of the news which we hear about "advanced" Christian countries of Europe and America and how the number of Christian believers there is not increasing or how there is a remarkable swing away from the Church and the Bible.

Considering the nature of the time and age in which we now live, this decline in Christianity is something which should be regarded with deep regret. This is because, whether Christian or not, we are each fundamentally aware in our heart that this age is a landmark period in our history, and the dramatic upheaval and change which is taking place around us from one day to the next is the concrete manifestation of how this age is moving shakily into the future. As a consequence, both humanity as a whole and each of us as individuals are compelled to make some kind of response or preparation.

It is an undeniable fact that in these modern times the power of those opposing God, which hinders man from making the necessary response or preparation (or in other words keeps people reluctant to venture into a brilliant new age), is ever increasing.

One example of this conspicuous Satanic movement in defiance of God is the calculated attempt to foster widespread belief in the theory of evolution (which is in fact an unfounded hypothesis) as a denial of the act of God's creation of the heavens and the earth.

This power of the forces against God is gathering momentum, both in our beloved country of Japan to which the far distant Gospel was brought, and in countries with a long Christian tradition. It is a solemn and distressing reality that many people have not made the response and preparation for moving into a new age.

As well as confuting the theory of evolution and exposing its fundamental errors, this book will help to elucidate the precepts of creation science in a very plain but persuasive style and will lead its audience to the Almighty God's wonderful and enlivening world of creation.

It is our hope that this book can play a part in the movement to "preach" the magnificent work of the creation of God, the almighty maker of all things, and to release many people at the crossroads of this age from the power of the forces of evil which, in order to spread the theory of evolution, masquerade as angels of light and servants of righteousness. In this way, we pray that this book will be used to make people join together in praise of God's creation and give thanks to Him.

We also hope that this book will signify, even if only as a token gesture, our thanks to those, beginning with people from English-speaking countries, who brought God's Good News even to this far distant land, and we trust that it will be a kind of reversed export of the Gospel from Japan.

We pray that all of us without exception can, with God's guidance and abundant blessing, make the response and preparation demanded by these times, and that this book will glorify God, who fulfilled his promise to bring the Gospel even to Japan, this land at the end of the earth.

Finally, we want to express great gratitude to the translator Mrs. Miriam Doi, Mr. Ken Yamada who helped translating, Dr. Henry M. Morris, president emeritus of the Institute for Creation Research (ICR), Dr. Masami Usami, Dr. Minoru Usami and Rev. Calton Elkins of Creation Science Association of Japan who encouraged us to publish this book.

In the name of our Lord Jesus Christ,

Arimasa Kubo (author)

Iwao Miyamoto (translator)
President, EastWest United Corporation

November 1, 2001

"The more thoroughly I conduct scientific research,
the more I believe that science excludes atheism."*

Lord Kelvin (British physicist, after whom the
Kelvin unit of absolute temperature was named.)

CHAPTER ONE

✦

The Birth of the Earth

1. The Earth: Suspended over Nothing

WE ALL have seen photographs of the earth taken from outer space. Everybody knows that the earth floats upon nothingness. But, the people of older times did not.

In India, for example, they used to think that the earth was on the back of a gigantic elephant, which was on the back of a gigantic turtle, which was on the backs of gigantic cobras, which were on the back of who-knows-what. And in Egypt, they used to think that the earth was resting on five gigantic pillars. But the Bible, which is the oldest book in the world, says:

"He (God) suspends the earth over nothing."

He (God) suspends the earth over nothing. (Job 26:7)

These words are from Job 26:7 in the Old Testament. They were written about three thousand years ago. And in those days there was, of course, no spacecraft, and nobody had gone out into space to look at the earth. But the Bible has been saying all along that the earth is suspended upon empty space, not on anything you can see with your eyes.

A lot of people are surprised to know that something like this is in the Bible. This is but one of the many surprising things the Bible says about the earth.

Some people think that the Bible is nothing but religious doctrine. Others think it is only a collection of myths. These people do not really know what the Bible says. Perhaps you, too, will be surprised as I point out a few more things.

2. Scientific Theory Has Been Changed

SCIENTIFIC THEORY used to disagree with the narrative in the first chapter of Genesis of the Bible about the early stages of the earth, and the formation of the oceans, atmosphere and land. And people used to laugh it off as "unscientific."

With the results of recent research, scientific theory has been vastly revised. Dr. Yasushi Kitano, professor at the Nagoya University Hydrospheric Research Laboratory of Japan says:

> "Until a few years ago, my colleagues and I would often agree that the so-called 'scientific' theories about things like the origin of the earth, oceans, atmosphere and land were more dreamy-eyed than scientific, but now, I think we can call them 'scientific.'"[1]

Now we know that what was once thought to be scientific theory was actually nothing more than fanciful imagination.

A lot of the theories that used to disagree with the Bible have either changed or have been discarded. In fact, the more developments and transitions there are, the closer scientific theory approaches the account in the Bible. I am not saying scientific theory "proves" that the Bible is right, for scientific theory is unstable. It is ever changing—while the Bible is never changing. Nothing can be proven with ever-changing theories.

This book is not scientific "proof," in the strict sense of the word, that the Bible is true. It is "news" about recent scientific theories, and how they are coming closer to the Bible.

Now, you are probably wondering what scientific discoveries I am talking about. As I present some of them here, let us think about the origin of the earth and the formation of the oceans, atmosphere and land.

3. The "Dust" That Formed the Earth

OF THE MANY theories about the birth of the earth, the one that, until recently, had been most believed for a long time was the one about a fireball that flew off from the sun and became the earth. According to this theory, hot gaseous substance flew off from the sun, condensed into a fireball, gradually cooled off, solidified, and became the earth.

This theory, however, because of its many unconvincing aspects, lost its credibility. Scientists later claimed that the earth was most likely formed from cold solid matter that clustered together.

"As with the theory of evolution of ape-becoming-man, the fireball-becoming-the-earth theory, too, had quietly slipped into the realm of common knowledge, with hardly anyone questioning it," say Dr. Shouji Ijiri (professor at Tokyo University) and Dr. Masao Minato (professor at Hokkaido

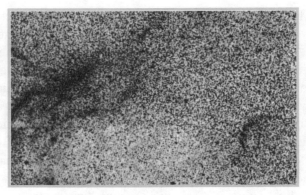

Countless specks of cold dust gathered together and formed the planets.

University) in their joint book *History of the Earth*. They added, "It was not until the end of the Second World War that scientists realized that the earth was most likely formed from cold solid matter that clustered together and later warmed up."[2]

In their book *Science of the Earth*, Dr. Hitoshi Takeuchi and Dr. Masaya Ueda (professors at Tokyo University) comment:

> "Since about 1940, the fireball-becoming-the-earth theory had become harder and harder to defend. It was then discarded and replaced by the 'Dust Theory' (low temperatural origin theory)."[3]

It is conceivable that this theory, which contends that the earth never was hot gaseous substance, but rather countless specks of cold dust that clustered together, is close to the description of the Bible.

There is no mention in the Bible that the earth was originally hot substance that flew off from the sun. In Proverbs 8:26, the Bible does say:

> "While He had not yet made…the first dust of the world…" (NASB)

So, it is conceivable that, in the very beginning, the earth was countless specks of cold "dust" that came into existence in space. The creation of the universe started with the creation of this "dust," which was the basic building block of matter. And later, the various atoms and molecules were formed; from this dust and its gathering must have come the earth.

4. Asteroids Collide and Combine

You Might be wondering exactly how the earth was formed out of this dust.

Of all the theories about the origin of the earth, the one which is currently the focus of world attention is the Matsui theory (by Dr. Takafumi Matsui, professor at Tokyo University).

Dr. Matsui thinks that, in the beginning, the solar system was nothing but a mist of cold dust. Much in the same way as snow falls and piles up, the dust, pulled in by a gravitational field, gently fell down from above and rose up from below toward the orbital plane of the solar system. The mist ended up condensed into the shape of a disc.

Then, there was a drastic change; the piled-up and over-tightly-packed particles suddenly broke out into countless clumps, or asteroids, each about 10 kilometers (or 6 miles) in diameter. These asteroids kept recklessly colliding and clashing into each other, sometimes getting smashed into pieces, but more often becoming part of the other asteroid.

And, like making a snowman, the cluster kept getting bigger and bigger. What was left after all this were a few

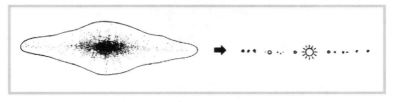

Asteroids collided, combined, and formed planets.

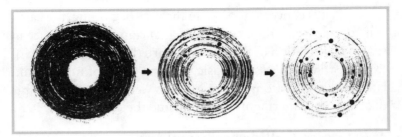

Simulation showing the process of asteroids growing.

gigantic asteroids that could be called celestial bodies; one of them, the earth; and the others, the other planets.[4]

Using computer simulation and other methods, scientists are now putting the Matsui theory to the test. The craters on the moon and the holes left by huge meteorites in the surface of the earth are thought to be the aftermath of collisions of the asteroids.

The intense heat produced by the colliding of the asteroids probably melted the surface of the primitive earth into a formless mass of mush. In Proverbs 8:24,25, the Bible says:

"...When there were no oceans...when there were no springs abounding with water; before the mountains were settled in place, before the hills..."

The craters on the moon could be the aftermath of the asteroids. The earth, too, has a lot of holes made by huge meteorites, but the atmosphere and the oceans have eroded them beyond recognition.

So the Bible, too, says that the earth was once without form—no mountains, no hills, and no oceans. But once the colliding of the asteroids came to an end, the surface of the earth gradually cooled off. And in that process, the oceans were born and the land took form.

5. The Heat Inside the Earth

GEOLOGISTS KNOW that the earth is made up of a crust (the outer layer), the mantle (the part below the crust), and a core. They often compare the earth to a boiled egg—the crust to the eggshell, the mantle to the white, and the core to the yolk. Geologists report that the substance in the mantle is very hot and slowly shifting.

The lava spewed out from volcanoes is magma, which is the rock and minerals melted by the heat of the mantle. At the core (outer core), they say, it is so hot that iron or nickel melts into molten mush. So the further inward you go, the hotter it gets; it is over 3000ºC at the core.

When and how did the inside of the earth get so hot? As the earth was developing, the bigger it became, the more gravitational pressure it received and the more compressed it got at the core. Today, it is estimated that the core receives the enormous amount of three billion millibars of pressure. The more pressure is applied to matter, the hotter it becomes. You have probably noticed that after you pump a few times, a bicycle pump gets warm. This is the heat generated from the compressed air.

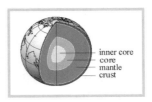

inner core
core
mantle
crust

The deeper inside the earth you go, the hotter it gets.

One of the sources of the heat at the earth's core is the enormous gravitational pressure it receives.

Another source is radioactivity. Radioactive elements, when giving off their share of radiation, expire and turn into different elements. This action generates heat. Since the beginning of creation, there have been enough radioactive elements in the earth's core to keep it hot indefinitely.

For reasons like these, it is conceivable that the inside of the earth was already hot in its early stages. According to Dr. Minoru Ojima, professor at Tokyo University, the earth's core had already been formed in its earliest stage. He says:

> "From the results of calculations to determine the origin of the atmosphere, we can surmise that the earth's core was formed immediately after the earth itself was born."[5]

The earth's core being formed at the outset means that the inside of the earth was hot right from the beginning. Through the intensification of this heat, the layered construction consisting of the core, the mantle, and the crust was formed. The earth grew up to a prearranged size and was formed in layers. We could call it "a living star." As the Bible says in Proverbs 8:29:

> "He (God) marked out the foundations of the earth."

6. The Earth—A Sphere

IN PROVERBS 8:27, the Bible says that God made the earth to be round:

> "When He inscribed a circle on the face of the deep…" (NASB)

The Hebrew word for "deep" is also used in Genesis 1:2 which describes the primitive earth. This word is translated into "oceans" there in many translations of the Bible, so it is probably safe to assume that "When He inscribed a circle on the face of the deep…" means that God planned the "oceans" or the horizon of the primitive earth to be round.

On the first day and the second day of God's Creation, the whole surface of the primitive earth was covered with oceans (as I will discuss later). That is why the Bible speaks here about the oceans. Also, in Job 26:10, the Bible says:

> "He has described a circle on the face of the waters at the boundary between light and darkness." (NRSV)

When the sun is above the horizon it is day, and when below, it is night. The horizon is "a boundary between light and darkness." God made the horizon to be round; in other words, God planned the earth to be round. In Isaiah 40:22, the Bible says:

> "He sits enthroned above the circle of the earth,
> and its people are like grasshoppers."

The expression "circle of the earth" used here is a direct translation from the Hebrew, the original language. When you look down at the earth from far above, you can see that it is in the shape of a circle.

And from the following passage from the Bible, we can see that it means not a flat circular shape, but rather a sphere:

> "When I (God) made a cloud its garment, and thick darkness its swaddling band…" (Job 38:9 NASB)

When God was creating the earth, he made for it a "swaddling band" of thick darkness. A swaddling band is a long strip of cloth which ancient Jewish people used for wrapping around a newborn baby. The thick darkness is portrayed as a swaddling band going around the newborn earth. From this, we can see that the "circle of the earth" is not a flat circular shape, but a sphere.

7. The Bible Mentions Earth's Tilted Axis

IN THE FIRST article of this chapter, I quoted the Bible verse, "he (God) suspends the earth over nothing." The complete verse goes like this:

> "He (God) spreads out the northern [skies] over empty space; he suspends the earth over nothing."
> (Job 26:7)

I imagine it must be difficult to grasp the meaning of the first half of this verse. The obscurity of the meaning reveals the inaccuracy of this translation. If we look at the Hebrew we can see that this English translation does not convey the exact meaning very well.

First of all, in Hebrew, the word translated into "northern skies" actually does not contain the meaning "skies," but only "north." (The King James Version translates it correctly however, "He stretcheth out the north...")

Secondly, the word translated "spreads out," in Hebrew, is *natah*. This word in other parts of the Bible, is translated "let down (your jar)" (Genesis 24:14), "leaning (wall)" (Psalms 62:3), "turn (either to the right hand or the left)" (Numbers 22:26), "follow (the multitude)" (Exodus 23:2), and "incline" (Judges 9:3).

So, *natah* has the meaning of leaning, slanting, or inclining from a basic position. If we exchange "northern skies" for "north" and "spreads out" for "incline," the same verse becomes: "God inclined the north..."

23.5 degrees

In relation to the earth's orbital plane, the earth's axis is tilted 23.5 degrees.

In relation to the earth's orbital plane, the earth's axis is tilted 23.5 degrees. In other words, just as the Bible describes, the earth's north is inclined.

God hung the earth in empty space and inclined the earth's north. Today we know that the four seasons we experience are the result of this tilt in the earth's axis.

It is amazing when you think that these verses were written about three thousand years ago.

8. The Water Planet

"THE BIG DIFFERENCE between Earth and the other planets is that Earth has a lot of water,"[6] says one scientist. The earth does have a great amount of water in the liquid state, not to mention its ice or water vapor.

In fact, 70 percent of the earth's surface is covered with seawater. Eighty percent of the bodies of the people who live on earth consist of water. Life cannot exist without water. No wonder scientists call the earth "the water planet."

Scientists used to think that the oceans were probably small at the beginning, and over a long period of time, slowly expanded into what they are today. But now they are convinced that large-scale oceans were there, right from the initial stages of the earth.

Geophysics professor at the University of Tokyo, Dr. Minoru Ojima says:

> "Most of the newest data suggests that in the initial stages of the earth's history, seawater of practically the same scale as today's already existed."[7]

The Bible, too, says that there were large-scale oceans in the initial stages. In Genesis 1:7, it says that "the water under the expanse (the sky)" was already there on the second day of creation.

The ocean was formed in the earth's initial stages.

The Bible says the oceans covered the whole surface of the earth at that time. This is possible because the earth's surface was smooth. (This will be explained later in this book.) So, in the initial stages, the oceans were already large-scale.

Many scientists used to think the chemical structure of the ocean in the initial stages was different than that of today. Professor Ojima, however, says that there was practically no difference:

> "Examining the chemical structure of sedimentary rock (rock formed from material that settled to the bottom of the water), we have found absolutely no intrinsic difference between the oldest and the newest. This tells us that the nature of the oceans of the initial stages was practically the same as that of today."[8]

9. The Atmosphere Materialized Suddenly

DID THE ATMOSPHERE gradually take shape over a very long period of time? Or did it materialize suddenly during the initial stages of the earth's development?

There is clear-cut proof that, in the same manner as the oceans, the atmosphere also materialized suddenly.

The atmosphere of today is 78 percent nitrogen and 21 percent oxygen. And in the remaining 1 percent, there are traces of carbon dioxide, water vapor, helium, hydrogen and other elements, but it is mostly argon.

Argon, having neither color nor smell, is usually unnoticed, but it is the third most abundant element in the atmosphere. And argon tells us a lot about the origin of the atmosphere.

With the results of recent research, we now know that during the initial stages of the earth's development, argon burst out from inside the minerals that made up the earth. Dr. Minoru Ojima, geophysics professor at Tokyo University, states:

> "Calculations about argon tell us that there was a sudden escape of gas from the minerals during the initial stages of the earth's history. And that it was a violent outburst."[9]

That is the way argon most likely materialized. Professor Ojima goes on to say that the other elements (nitrogen, etc.) of the atmosphere materialized the same way:

> "The same results can be expected for nitrogen, water vapor, and the other elements of the atmosphere.... Over 80 percent of the argon, having come out in a sudden outburst, means that, although there may have been differences in degree, other volatile matter (matter that evaporates at normal temperatures and pressures), too, came out in a sudden outburst."[10]

The atmosphere materialized suddenly.

The Bible, too, says that the atmosphere materialized in a sudden outburst. It says that there was no atmosphere like today's on the first day of creation, but that there was on the second day:

> "So God made the expanse and separated the water under the expanse from the water above it. And it was so. God called the expanse 'sky.' And there was evening, and there was morning—the second day." (Genesis 1:7,8)

The "sky" (atmosphere) suddenly appeared on the second day of creation.

10. The Atmosphere and the Oceans Have the Same Origin

YOU ARE probably wondering just how the atmosphere and the oceans suddenly materialized. According to Dr. Takafumi Matsui, professor at Tokyo University, the oceans and the atmosphere emerged together.

He maintains that the newly born earth was at first covered with a great amount of water vapor atmosphere. This atmosphere, containing mostly water vapor, was a lot different than today's. But it did contain most of the basic elements of today's atmosphere. This water vapor was at first inside the minerals of the asteroids that later formed the earth.

This might be easier to picture if you think about meteorites. At first glance, they do not look like they have any water in them at all. But when you examine them more carefully, they are surprisingly watery. When the asteroids were colliding and combining and forming the earth, the water vapor escaped from the melted minerals of the asteroids.

And after the earth had been formed, what was left around it was a thick atmosphere of the water vapor. "Over 80% of the volatile matter from the minerals was water," says Dr. Matsui. He then added:

> "So it is safe to conclude that the atmosphere of the primitive earth was the atmosphere mostly made of water vapor."[11]

The primitive earth was covered with water vapor atmosphere.

The primitive earth was covered with the atmosphere whose main ingredient was water vapor. The bulk of this water vapor later cooled off and turned into a deluge of rain, and became the vast oceans.

At first, there was the water vapor atmosphere. Later it was divided, and became the atmosphere of nitrogen, argon, and others, and below it became the oceans. By scientific calculations, it is known that the amount of all the water around the surface of the earth today (1.5×10^{21} kg, most of it is sea water) is almost the same as the calculated amount of the water vapor of the water vapor atmosphere which seems to have been formed on the primitive earth.

The Bible, too, says that the earth was covered with a great amount of water on the first day of creation. The Bible says about the first day:

> "In the beginning God created the heavens and the earth. Now the earth was formless and empty, darkness was over the surface of the deep, and the Spirit of God was hovering over the waters." (Genesis 1:1,2)

The "waters" of the primitive earth must have been the water vapor atmosphere. This water vapor atmosphere was divided on the second day of creation into the sky and the oceans.

> "And God said, 'Let there be an expanse between the waters to separate water from water.' So God made the expanse and separated the water under the expanse from the water above it. And it was so. God called the expanse 'sky.' And there was evening, and there was morning—the second day." (Genesis 1:6-8)

I will discuss "the water above the expanse" later. This is the water vapor canopy that existed in the upper atmosphere of the earth before the Noah's great flood. The outermost layer of the water vapor atmosphere did not become part of the deluge, and remained where it was. Below this were formed the "sky" and the oceans. "Expanse" means the sky or the atmosphere made up of nitrogen, argon, and other elements. "The water under the expanse" means the newly formed oceans.

Now we know that scientific theory again comes closer to the Bible. Science states that the atmosphere and the oceans emerged together. The Bible states that these were formed on the same day—the second day of creation.

Science says that the atmosphere and the oceans both came from the water vapor atmosphere of the primitive earth. The Bible says that both came from the vast amount of "waters" that covered the primitive earth. A thick atmosphere and large-scale oceans already existed in the earth's initial stages.

Even today, hot springs and the gas from volcanoes are slowly increasing the amount of water above the earth's surface.

Even today, things like hot springs and the gas from volcanoes are slowly increasing the amount of water above the earth's surface. The gas from volcanoes is mostly water vapor. And all over the ocean bed, there are volcanoes that are releasing hot water.

In short, the water that makes up the oceans was originally embedded in the minerals of the asteroids and later in the earth itself. The water burst out from the inside. In Job 38:8, the Bible says:

"Who shut up the sea behind doors when it burst forth from the womb?"

So the Bible, too, says that water came out from the inside, or the "womb," of the earth.

11. Why There Is an Atmosphere

NOT ALL celestial bodies have atmospheres. Not all planets have one. The moon does not have one.

The diameter of the moon is about one-quarter of the earth's. It does not have much mass. Its gravity is only 17 percent of the earth's—not enough to hold down an atmosphere.

If the earth were 10 percent smaller, there would be no life on it. (From the New Life League pamphlet "Have You Been Brainwashed?")

The earth has an atmosphere because it has enough mass and enough gravity to hold one down. If the earth were smaller, it probably would not have an atmosphere. Research Scientist Dr. Duane T. Gish, former head of the biological-medicine division at Upjohn pharmaceutical company, comments:

> "When you stop to think about the size of the earth, you realize just how perfect its mass and its measurements are. If its 12,800 kilometer (8000 miles) diameter were 11,500 kilometers (7200 miles), the weakening of the atmosphere would turn almost the whole world into a wilderness of snow and ice."[12]

If the earth were 10 percent smaller, there would not be any life on it. In Job 38:5, the Bible says:

> "Who decided how large it (the earth) would be? Who stretched the measuring line over it?" (TEV)

When we think about the earth's mass or its size, we can see that it was all in the Creator's master plan.

12. The Land Rose Up from the Ocean

HOW AND WHEN did the land take form? Let us start with the old riddle: which came first, the land or the oceans.

In other words, when the water vapor atmosphere sent down the deluge of rain, did the water settle down into the low spots of an uneven surface, forming both the oceans and continents right from start? Or was the surface smooth, with no low spots, giving the water no set areas to settle down into, forming one big ocean with no continents? In their joint book, *History of the Earth* Shouji Ijiri and Masao Minato say:

> "A lot of the answers to the mysteries of the oceans are hidden in the land. Because that is what land is—former ocean beds."[13]

So, continents were once ocean beds. In the same book, they continue:

> "A mountain can not be formed unless it had been part of the ocean bed. Over a long period of time, material like mud, sand and stones settles down and piles up several thousands, or some-times several tens of thousands of meters high on the deeply dipped ocean bed. These are the pre-conditions for orogenic (mountain making) movements.
>
> And during the following geological eras, such an ocean bed becomes an area of violent rise and mountain making.... After that, the area becomes a stable landmass which will no more be an area of mountain making. This is the way a continent is formed."[14]

The land rose up from the ocean.

In other words, geophysicists think that land was once part of the ocean bed that was piled up with materials, and was pushed up through the surface of the ocean by forces inside the earth.

The Bible says that the earth did not have any land at first, but was completely covered with ocean, and on the third day, the land came out from the ocean:

> "And God said, 'Let the water under the sky be gathered to one place, and let dry ground appear': And it was so. God called the dry ground 'land,' and the gathered waters he called 'seas'. And God saw that it was good." (Genesis 1:9,10)

So, at first, there was just ocean. Then, with the shifting in the mantle, the ocean bed bulged out through the surface of the water and became "dry ground." The water then gathered into the lower part of the earth's surface, and the land and the ocean became separate. As the Bible says:

"the earth was formed out of water and by water."
(II Peter 3:5)

13. Oxygen Came into the Atmosphere

OXYGEN IS 21 percent of the atmosphere. Without it we would not be alive. Nor would any animal. Where did this oxygen come from? Scientists believe that in the early atmosphere, there was no oxygen that was uncombined with other elements.

I mentioned earlier that the atmosphere materialized from the asteroids and from the inside of the earth. But if you examine a meteorite, there is hardly any oxygen inside it.

There is no atmospheric oxygen on Venus. There is none on Mars. In fact, aside from Earth, there is no atmospheric oxygen on any of the planets of the solar system, even though they may have an atmosphere.

Oxygen, not coming from the asteroids nor from inside the earth, is different from the other elements. In *History of the Earth*, Hitoshi Takeuchi and Akiho Miyashiro say:

> "There was virtually no oxygen in this atmosphere long ago.... It was the arrival of the plants and their photosynthesis that brought about the large amounts of oxygen. In this respect, oxygen has a completely different origin than the other elements of the atmosphere."[15]

According to these scientists, it was plants that gave us oxygen. The Bible says that God made the atmosphere on the second day of creation. And then, on the third day, after making the land, he made the plant kingdom on the land and on the ocean bed.

> "Then God said, 'Let the land produce vegetation; seed-bearing plants and trees on the land that

bear fruit with seed in it, according to their various kinds.' And it was so. The land produced vegetation: plants bearing seed according to their kinds and trees bearing fruit with seed in it according to their kinds. And God saw that it was good. And there was evening, and there was morning—the third day." (Genesis 1:11-13)

Plants, taking in carbon dioxide and giving off oxygen, were created on "the third day." Giving off oxygen by plants began on the third day of creation. This is how the large amount of oxygen was brought into the atmosphere. And because the plants themselves were made of all kinds of edible organic matter, the stage was set for the coming of animals and man.

14. The Elements in the Early Atmosphere

In 1953, Stanley Loyd Miller of America, performed that famous experiment on the origin of life.

He mixed methane, ammonia, water vapor, hydrogen, and some other gases together. He reported that after sending an electric current through it for a few days, he ended up with amino and other organic acids. In Russia, too, they duplicated the experiment, and admitted that it does work. This was sensational news to all the people researching the origin of life in view of evolution theory.

Out of inorganic matter, he had succeeded in synthesizing organic matter, which is the basic material of life. So with this knowledge, believers in the theory of evolution started saying that the atmosphere of the early earth must have been one containing a lot of methane, ammonia, hydrogen, and other gases.

They call this "the deoxidized (oxygen reducing) atmosphere." And they call the theory that life started evolving in such an atmosphere "the deoxidized atmosphere theory."

Accordingly they started calling today's atmosphere "the oxidized atmosphere."

Considering that today's atmosphere has nitrogen, carbon dioxide, water vapor, oxygen, argon, and other gases, many scientists say that there is no way the so-called deoxidized atmosphere could ever have existed. But supporters of the theory argue that the deoxidized atmosphere gradually, over the ages, evolved into the atmosphere of today.

However, Dr. Yasushi Kitano, professor at the Nagoya University Hydrospheric Research Laboratory of Japan, comments:

> "As always, there are a lot of supporters of the deoxidized atmosphere theory among evolutionists in America and other countries. And, it seems that most of the biologists researching the origin of life, Japanese included, support the theory, too. The reason for this might be that it is very difficult to synthesize amino acid from oxidized elements like carbon dioxide, nitrogen, or water vapor."[16]

Most believers in the theory of evolution are inclined to be tenacious believers in the deoxidized atmosphere theory. But the proof is thin. Professor Kitano adds:

> "Most scientists with backgrounds in physics or chemistry in Japan—Teishi Matsuo, Mikio Shimizu, Minoru Ojima, Fujio Egami, and myself included—support the theory that life began in an atmosphere containing the same elements as today's."[17]

Further, Professor Kitano shows some weighty facts which support the thought that life began in the oxidized atmosphere, not in an imagined deoxidized one. For example, among the rocks of the oldest possible category, limestone was discovered. This alone disproves the deoxidized atmosphere theory. Limestone requires carbon dioxide to form.

So the existence of limestone in those days tells us that carbon dioxide was in the air. With the multitude of theoretical arguments against the deoxidized atmosphere theory, it is easy to see why a lot of scientists have discarded it.

From a Biblical viewpoint, too, it is not conceivable that an atmosphere of methane, ammonia, and hydrogen slowly evolved into today's atmosphere. Various scientific facts tell us that the atmosphere of the early earth already contained the same elements as today's.

Chapter Two

The Creation
of the Universe

1. The Creator of the Universe

Discoverer of the law of gravitation, the great English scientist, Sir Isaac Newton, once hired a mechanical engineer to make a model of the solar system. It was a sophisticated apparatus with sprockets and chains making each planet rotate and revolve around the sun in high precision. He had it set on a big table in his living room.

One day, when Sir Newton was sitting in the room reading, his atheist scientist friend dropped by. The friend, seeing the apparatus on the table, started turning the crank that set it in motion. Seeing all the planets rotating and revolving in harmony, he was impressed and asked, "Who made this?"

Sir Newton, without raising his eyes from his book, answered, "Nobody made it."

The friend asked again, "I don't think you understood my question. I'm asking you who made this."

Sir Newton raised his face from his book, and with a serious face explained that some odds and ends just gathered together and that by sheer chance ended up in that shape, and that nobody made it. But the atheist friend, beginning to lose his composure, exclaimed, "Isaac! You're insulting me. Any fool can see that someone made this. And what a genius that someone is! I'm asking you who it is."

Sir Newton put his book down at his side, got up from his chair, put a hand on his friend's shoulder and said:

"This is nothing but a crude model of the far more glorious solar system. And I'm sure you know the natural laws that govern it. When I tell you that this crude toy took shape of its own accord, without a designer or a maker, you don't believe me. Yet, you say that the real solar system, in all its splendor, came about without a designer or a maker. How did you come to this conclusion? Explain the inconsistency."

This is the way Sir Newton convinced his friend that behind the universe there is a great creator who has intelligence. In his book *Principia*, Isaac Newton wrote:

> "Unless you suppose that the sun, planets and comets of our marvelous solar system came into existence under the plan and control of an almighty and intelligent being, there is no way to explain it…. The Almighty God is eternal, boundless and perfect."*

He believed that the universe was created by the Almighty God, who cannot be seen with our eyes. And that it is under the control of this Almighty God that the universe exists. About his research, he said, "I am frolicking on the beach of the ocean of truth."* He meant that, through scientific inquiry he was pursuing "God's Truth."

Albert Einstein, the man who came up with the theory of relativity, and is reputed to have been the greatest scientist of the twentieth century is known to have said:

> "I am a man looking for 'God's Footprints' within His creation."

It was the desire to know God better that inspired Dr. Einstein to make a scientific inquiry into the realm of nature.

In fact, most of the greatest scientists of all time were believers in God the Creator. In the long list you will find Kelvin and Kepler, Maxwell and Millikan, Boyle and Dawson, Compton and Copernicus, J. Fleming, Fabre and Faraday, Pascal, Pasteur and Planck, Galilei, Linnaeus and Virchow, to name a few.

They were all solid believers in the God of the Bible who created the heavens and the earth. And as any science historian will tell you, their great achievements were the result of the desire to better understand the construction of God's creation.

Michael Faraday unveils his experiments to the public. He strongly believed that creationism should be taught to all people.

2. The Realm of Nature

THE FLOWERS gently swaying in the field; the brook running through the plateau; the countless stars in the night sky of the countryside; the ocean of clouds seen from the top of a mountain. There is grandeur, splendor, and loftiness in nature. According to Romans 1:20:

> "...since the creation of the world God's invisible qualities—his eternal power and divine nature— have been clearly seen, being understood from what has been made..."

This means that the grandeur, splendor, and loftiness of nature are actually manifestations of God's eternal power and divine nature. That is why so many people who have made deep scientific inquiry into the universe ended up believing that there is a Creator.

The universe, under its laws of physics and chemistry, stays in perfect order. And when you examine it, you are fascinated by its beauty and magnificence. Albert Einstein used to say:

> "There is mathematical beauty in the laws of the universe."

The 1933 Nobel Prize winning physicist and mathematician Paul A. M. Dirac of England said in an article in *Scientific American*:

> "God is a super mathematician. The mathematics he used when he was making the universe was extremely advanced."*

All of the scientific laws that keep the universe in order are truly magnificent. And it was God who decided them. Just

God's eternal power and divine nature are perceived in the realm of nature.

as the 1927 Nobel Prize winning American scientist Arthur Holly Compton was known to say:

> "The perfect order of the universe proves that the most profound words ever spoken are true; 'In the beginning God created the heavens and the earth' (Genesis 1:1)."*

When we look at the universe, we can see that there definitely was a designer, a builder, and that there is a preserver. If the universe exists, then God exists. Through the realm of nature, which he made, we can sense his eternal power and his divine nature.

At the 1948 American Physicists' Convention, Robert A. Millikan, who won a Nobel Prize for his research in electricity and cosmic rays, was speaking about an entity that lives behind the scenes of the universe. He called it "the Almighty Master Builder."* He went on to conclude:

"The materialism, which is the thought that physical matter is the only reality and that everything can be explained in terms of it, is absolute nonsense."*

The great German scientist, Max Planck, said:

"Unless you assume that there is an intelligent, supreme creator, it would be impossible to explain the formation of the universe."

There have been many believers in God among the scientists in the hall of fame. And among the top scientists of today, too, the number is growing. In America, according to a survey, before World War II, only 35 percent of the scientists believed in God the Creator. But today, 60 percent believe.

I have heard people say, "Anyone with scientific knowledge would never believe in God." But people who think like this are the ones without the scientific knowledge of which they boast. In fact, it was through scientific research that a lot of people came to be believers.

Some people declare, "There is no such thing as God!" But the Bible says, "The fool says in his heart, 'There is no God.'" (Psalm 14:1)

Belief in God is not unscientific or irrational. It is just the opposite. It is reasonable to think that the universe was brought into existence out of nothingness according to the master plan of the Almighty God.

3. The Universe Came Out of Nothingness

ABOUT THE origin of the universe, some people say, "If all that Bible stuff is true, how do you explain 'The Big Bang Theory'?"

The big bang theory has attained a degree of popularity lately. How should we consider it? Does it really deny the thought of the creation of the universe by God?

This theory is the thought that the universe came into existence explosively and is still expanding. There are several different opinions among Christian and non Christian scientists concerning the big bang theory, but here, let's take a look at some interesting points in the theory.

Before the big bang theory, not many people supposed that there was a beginning. The "Theory of Steady State Universe," which is the thought that the universe has no beginning and no end, was more than a theory; it was in the realm of common sense. Even the Buddhist teachings of "No-Beginning-No-End" of the universe had the ring of profundity. The big bang theory denied the thought and gave evidences that there had been a beginning of the universe. In this sense, the Big Bang Theory is close to the idea of creation.

At first, advocates of the big bang theory thought that in the beginning, there was a small point that was probably stuffed with super-dense matter. And that it exploded and became the universe. Later, they realized that such super-dense matter could never have existed, and that there was probably nothing at all in the point. The revised Big Bang Theory is that the universe came out of "nothingness."

Scientists have discovered that light and matter have dual natures. One is that they behave as though they are composed of particles like electrons, neutrons, and so on. The other is of a seemingly contradictory nature; they behave as though they are waves or fluctuations. They call this "the quantum theory."

According to quantum theory, a vacuum is not a condition in which nothing occurs, but is like a tunnel in which fluctuations can draw atomic particles into existence. A leading American scientist says:

"The universe came out of nothingness of free state in the sense of quantum theory."[*1]

Some interesting points about the "Big Bang Theory": firstly, that there was a beginning to the universe and, secondly, that (as can be seen in more recent theories) the universe was born out of nothingness.

And in the 1984 May issue of *Scientific American*, it states:

"It was fluctuations of vacuum in the sense of quantum mechanics that brought the universe into existence."*2

So, according to the revised big bang theory, in the beginning there was nothing. And with the "big bang" of the time and space continuum, the universe appeared and came into existence. Look what the Bible has been saying:

"...the God who gives life to the dead and calls things that are not as though they were." (Romans 4:17)

"Lift your eyes and look to the heavens: Who created all these? He who brings out the starry host one by one, and calls them each by name. Because of his great power and mighty strength, not one of them is missing." (Isaiah 40:26)

Here we can see that all of the celestial bodies including the earth were led out like an army from nothingness into existence by God's "power." There is a Bible that translates the word "power" as "energy." This is interesting. Today's scientists say that, using Einstein's theory ($E=mc^2$), you can change matter into energy and you can change energy into matter.

With this in mind, it is reasonable to think that God, who is abundant in energy, changed energy into matter when he brought the universe into existence. The Bible also says:

"he (God) who created the heavens and stretched them out..." (Isaiah 42:5)

So when the big bang theory says that the universe came out of nothingness and was "stretched out" explosively, it is close to what the Bible says. It does not deny the thought of the creation of the universe by God.

Furthermore, among many religious scriptures and myths in the world, only the Bible states truly that the universe came out of nothingness. There are many myths, religious scriptures, and sutras about the beginning of the universe. But in every one of them, substance was already in existence before creation.

In his book *Mythology Mysteries: Creation of Earth and Heavens*, Atsuhiko Yoshida describes the different types of myths. There is the one in which the universe hatches from a gigantic egg; there is the one in which a god orders water birds to go the bottom of the ocean and get soil and little by little make the land.

There is one in which a god and goddess stir the ocean with a pike and magically form the land with the drops. There is another in which the body of a dead giant becomes the world. And the list goes on.

In every myth, substance had already existed before creation. The people of ancient times must have been rather placid not to question where the substance came from. But in Genesis 1:1, the Bible says:

> "In the beginning God created the heavens and the earth."

The Bible says that creation was "in the beginning," and that before creation, substance was non-existent. Our universe was created by "the God who…calls things that are not as though they were." (Romans 4:17)

4. Matter Becomes Activated

AFTER GOD brought into being what did not exist and started creating the universe, how did he go about putting the laws of nature into operation?

> "In the beginning God created the heavens and the earth. Now the earth was formless and empty, darkness was over the surface of the deep, and the Spirit of God was hovering over the waters."
> (Genesis 1:1,2)

This passage tells us that while the earth and the rest of the universe were still in chaos, an invisible entity (the Spirit of God) was activating and setting everything into order. One meaning of the words "Spirit of God" is "origin of power." All forms of energy came from the Spirit of God, as He was "hovering over the waters."

The Hebrew word that was translated into "hovering" (or "move" in other translations) was used in situations such as when hens move or flap their wings up and down and sit on their eggs to warm waiting for them to hatch.

So when the Spirit of God was moving and hovering over the universe, he was sending energy to it and warming it. Dr. Henry M. Morris, President Emeritus of the Institute for Creation Research of America comments:

> "In modern scientific terminology, the best translation would probably be 'vibrated.'.... It is significant that the transmission of energy in the operations of the cosmos is in the form of waves—light waves, heat waves, sound waves, and so forth. In fact (except for the nuclear forces which are involved in the structure of matter itself), there are only two fundamental types of forces that operate on matter—the gravitational forces and the forces of the electromagnetic spectrum. All are associated with 'fields' of activity and with transmission by wave motion."[3]

By vibrating, the Spirit of God was creating waves of energy that made up the universe and activated it into order.

After calling the universe into existence and activating it, God's creation was completed on the seventh day.

> "Thus the heavens and the earth were completed in all their vast array. By the seventh day God had finished the work he had been doing; so on the seventh day he rested from all his work."
> (Genesis 2:1,2)

God had been supplying energy to create and to form the universe during the first six days of creation, but after he had finished his work by the seventh day, he fixed physical laws and chemical laws to entrust them with the movement of the universe. So, we can think that God has not supplied any new energy after that, and the total amount of energy in the universe became constant.

Concerning energy, we know the law of constancy of energy—the most basic principle of physics. Even though energy (including matter, which is actually a form of energy) changes in physical or chemical form, the total amount of energy in the universe never changes.

According to this law of constancy of energy, the total amount of energy in the universe has been constant, and has a specific value. We can say that the Bible verses "completed," "finished the work," and "rested" tell us about the law of constancy of energy.

5. Light Before the Sun!?

"GOD SAID, 'Let there be light,' and there was light. God saw that the light was good, and he separated the light from the darkness. God called the light 'day,' and the darkness he called 'night.' And there was evening, and there was morning—the first day." (Genesis 1:3-5)

> "God made two great lights—the greater light to govern the day and the lesser light to govern the night. He also made the stars. God set them in the expanse of the sky to give light on the earth, to govern the day and the night, and to separate light from darkness…. And there was evening, and there was morning—the fourth day." (Genesis 1:16-19)

You might think it strange that God made light on the first day of creation, but did not make the sun until the fourth day. How can there be light without a sun, which is the source of light?

This is not strange if we look at what today's scientists say about the origin of the sun.

We can discover the constituent materials of a star by examining its light spectrum.

They say that there is more hydrogen in the universe than any other element. Hydrogen has a simpler structure than any other element; a hydrogen atom is made up of only one proton and one electron. The second most abundant element in the universe is helium, which has the second simplest structure.

Together hydrogen and helium constitute about 98 percent of all the matter in the universe. So all of the rest of the elements together constitute only about 2 percent. Things like light spectra from stars tell us that this is so. Each element has its own light spectrum. So by examining the light spectrum from a star, we can find out what elements there are.

The general theory is that in the beginning, the sun was nothing more than a haze of gas. It was the mutual gravitational pull of atoms of hydrogen and some other elements, and molecules, too, that formed this haze.

Explaining the theory, Dr. Shinya Obi, professor at Tokyo University, says that it was the gravitation of the haze itself that made it condense. And when the condensing had reached a certain point, it burst out into bright light:

"On the inside, the haze of gas had already reached a density where the condensing had stopped. But in the outer limits of the haze, the density and temperature were still low. The particles from the outer limits fell inwards, at supersonic speed, violently colliding with the highly dense insides. This produced shock waves that were sent back to the outer limits."

"The passing of the shock waves through the haze," he continues, "created heat. Even at the outer limits, it was almost 4,000 degrees Celsius. It was this heat that made the bright light burst out from the haze. The size of the haze was bigger than the orbit of today's Mercury."[4]

So that is how, after reaching a high enough temperature, "the bright light burst out from the haze" of gas. And it was indeed a very bright light.

The glowing haze of gas was much different than the sun of today. At that stage, nuclear fusion had not yet started; today's sun gets its energy through nuclear fusion. The haze was also much bigger than today's sun. You could call it the "pre-sun."

They say that, compared to the length of time the sun has been here, it did not take long for the haze to condense even more, getting down to the size the sun is today. After the condensing was completed, there was enough heat on the inside for nuclear fusion to start. Dr. Obi says:

"This condensing generated even more heat on the inside, ultimately reaching over 10,000,000 degrees Celsius. And then, nuclear fusion with hydrogen started…and the sun was born."[5]

The energy from nuclear fusion keeps the sun shining. Its light is stabilized, and it shines on us everyday. It is probably safe to say that the sun was not truly born until the continual energy from nuclear fusion was activated.

We cannot prove beyond a doubt that this is the exact way that God created light and then later created the sun. But it is food for thought. The Bible says that in the beginning, the earth was "formless and desolate." So it is probably safe to think that the sun, too, was nothing more than a "formless and desolate" cluster of particles.

If the theory is true, then, on the first day of creation, it was the light from this "pre-sun" or haze of glowing gas that gave the earth, which was already rotating, the first day and night. It is conceivable, then, that on the fourth day of creation, the condensing of the haze was completed, and with its nuclear fusion, it became the sun as we know it, that continues to shine indefinitely.

In Hebrew, the original language, *asah*, the word for "make" from the statement, "God made two great lights" in Genesis 1:16, usually means "to make something from existing material." For example, the Hebrew word *asah* is used in "make for yourself an ark of cypress wood" in Genesis 6:14. Here, *asah* is translated into "make," which means that Noah makes an ark of cypress wood. Cypress wood is the existing material. We conclude that the meaning of "asah" is to make something from existing material. (You can see the same thing in Genesis 18:6, 27:4, 31:46, 33:17, 35:1, and many other places.)

Light was created before the formation of today's sun.

Asah is used as man's work as well as God's work. When it is used as man's work, it always means to make something from existing material. When it is used as God's work, sometimes it means to create from nothing, and sometimes to make something from existing material.

The Hebrew word *bara* from Genesis 1:1 which is translated "create" is always used as God's work, never as man's work. It means to create from nothing. (You can see this by checking the concordance.)

It is conceivable that, on the fourth day of creation, God did not suddenly bring the sun into existence out from nothingness, but rather, made it out of existing material. Before God made the sun, a pre-sun, in other words, the material that he used to make it, was already there.

On the first day of creation when God commanded, "Let there be light" (Genesis 1:3), light appeared from the pre-sun at the center of the solar system. This gave the earth day and night.

According to the Bible, "there was evening and there was morning" (Genesis 1:5) since the first day of creation, because light came from the pre-sun at the center of the solar system and the earth was already rotating. On the fourth day, God made the pre-sun into the sun of today.

The "light" of Genesis 1:3 is not the light which the big bang theory states filled the entire newborn universe. It could not have given the earth evening and morning. The "light" of Genesis 1:3 gave the earth evening and morning. The reason is that the light came from the center of the solar system and the primitive earth was already rotating.

That seems to be the way the sun, which plays the most important role in creating the environment necessary for life on earth, came into being. And even today, the earth, orbiting this sun, continues to receive the sun's light and heat.

6. Earth's Magnetic Field: Our Protection from Solar Wind

SUNSHINE IS essential to all life on the earth. But not all that comes from the sun is beneficial. There is destructive "solar wind." Solar wind is not the wind that blows around inside our atmosphere; it is a high-speed stream of dangerously charged atomic particles that radiates from the sun.

During America's *Apollo* space mission on the moon, vigilant observation of the sun was maintained at every second. It was this solar wind that they were so watchful about. Whenever there is an eruption of hydrogen gas on the sun's surface (a solar flare), a powerful solar wind is blown off.

Its radiation is strong enough to go right through a space suit and kill the man inside. If this horrific solar wind were to reach the earth's surface in full force, it would annihilate all life. Fortunately, however, the earth's magnetic field and atmosphere protect us from it.

Today we know that the earth is one gigantic magnet. The reason, according to the weightiest scientific theory today, is that there is an electric current inside the earth, making it so.

The intense heat inside the earth melts all the iron of the mantle and of the outer core. As the earth spins round and round on its axis, the molten iron, which is a conductor of electricity, becomes a natural dynamo. This dynamo generates electricity inside the earth. And with this electricity running through it, the earth becomes an electromagnet. This in turn, generates the magnetic field around the earth.

This magnetic field catches the dangerously charged atomic particles from the sun and cages them in. Surrounding the earth, there is a donut-shaped zone called the "Van Allen belt." The inside of this belt is swarming with the radioactive atomic particles caught by the earth's magnetic field.

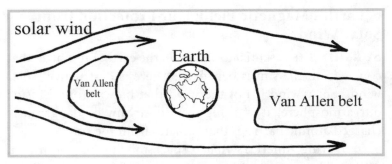

The earth's magnetic field protects the earth from the harmful effects of solar wind.

The radioactivity there is so intense that spacecraft avoid going through it. That is the way the earth's magnetic field protects life from solar wind. Our atmosphere too, in the same way, catches destructive atomic particles and keeps them from reaching the earth's surface.

The Bible says that on the first day of creation, "there was evening, and there was morning." This means that right from Day One, the earth was already spinning on its axis, generating electricity inside, and sending out the magnetic field.

We can see that great care was taken to make the earth a suitable place for life.

7. Heliocentricity Theory: Established by Christians

EARTH: A member of the solar system, it orbits the sun 150 million kilometers (93 million miles) away from it. In volume, it is 1.3 million times smaller than the sun; a small planet.

It is a well-known fact that in the Middle Ages, there were two opposing scientific theories about the relationship between the earth and the sun. One was "the theory of geocentricity" and the other was "the theory of heliocentricity."

The geocentricity theory was the idea that the earth was the center of the universe and that the sun orbited the earth. On the other hand, the heliocentricity theory was the idea that it was the sun at the center and that the earth was doing the orbiting.

A lot of people think that the Bible advocates the theory of geocentricity; it does not. The theory was just what people used to believe back in the Middle Ages—not anything from the Bible.

In the seventeenth century, Galileo Galilei met a lot of opposition when he was advocating the theory of heliocentricity. People back then were convinced that the earth was stationary and that the sun was orbiting the earth. Galilei never disagreed with any Bible teachings. In fact, he was a Christian; he believed what the Bible taught. He was so much a believer in God that he said:

> "Bring me a microscope, and I will rip atheism to tatters."

He wrote two letters explaining that the theory of heliocentricity does not contradict the Bible—one to the Grand Duchess Christina and the other to his friend Castigli.

And even before Galilei, back in the sixteenth century, the great astronomer Nicolaus Copernicus was already advocating the theory of heliocentricity. He too was a zealous Christian who believed that God created the universe.

In those days, people used to believe the scientific theory of the astronomer Claudius Ptolemy that the sun orbits the earth. For Copernicus, the idea was just too twisted, tangled, and entangled. And he noticed that too much was left unexplained. He then declared:

> "I couldn't imagine that God, who can do anything to perfection, would make a universe that ended up in such a mess."[6]

(From above) Copernicus, Galilei, and Kepler. Those who established the heliocentricity theory were Christians. They believed in God, the creator of the universe.

It was Copernicus' belief in God that would not let him accept Ptolemy's theory. His own idea, in which the earth orbits the sun, was born as the result of this. Zealous scientific research combined with the belief that God created the universe led both Copernicus and Galilei to the natural conclusion that it is the earth that orbits the sun, and not the other way around.

Most of the first chapter of Genesis deals with the earth, so some people think the Bible teaches that the earth is the axial point of the universe. But their interpretation is mistaken. The chapter is written in such a way that it puts you at a place where you can "observe" the earth being created. In other words, from an "earth-viewpoint."

In a formal discussion about astronomy, nobody would say, "The sun rises in the east and sets in the west." But you can use that figure of speech in ordinary conversation and nobody would think that you meant the sun is literally orbiting the earth. It is only natural for us to express ourselves from an earth-viewpoint because we are experiencing life here on the earth.

In the Bible, the Psalmist says, "From the rising of the sun to the place where it sets, the name of the Lord is to be praised" (Psalm 113:3). The Psalmist is not implying that the sun comes out of the earth someplace in the distance and sets somewhere else. Nor is he implying that the sun is orbiting the earth. He is simply saying, from an earth-viewpoint, that the name of the Lord is to be praised everywhere.

And it is because we live on the earth and have an earth-viewpoint that the first chapter of Genesis, written for us, centers its focus on Earth, rather than, say, Neptune, or a star in some distant galaxy. Nowhere in the Bible does it say that the sun is orbiting the earth.

Both Galilei and Copernicus had no trouble accepting the idea that the earth was not the central point of the universe but only one of the many planets revolving around the sun. They both believed the teachings of the Bible—that spiritually the center of the universe is God, not man.

That is why they could not accept Ptolemy's idea that the earth was the center of the solar system and of the rest of the universe. And that is why they ultimately did realize that the earth was a planet orbiting the sun.

History books say that when the great German astronomer Johannes Kepler discovered the laws of planetary orbits (Kepler's laws), being overwhelmed with emotion, he dropped to his knees and praised the Lord God.

The heliocentricity theory was established by these men; they were all Christians.

8. Earth—The Special Planet

COMPARED TO the countless celestial bodies in the galaxy, what exactly is our Earth? To answer that question, first, we have to ask what kind of star the sun is, since Earth is a member of its system. Having 1.3 million times the volume of the earth, the sun is enormous. But how does it compare with the other stars scattered throughout the galaxy?

Astrophysicists say that, according to modern research, the sun is about average in size and brightness compared with the other stars. The sun is just one of the countless stars (fixed stars) in the night sky; it just looks bigger because it is closer.

Astrophysicist Dr. Takeo Hatanaka says:

> "Excluding the planets, all the stars we see in the night sky are exactly like the sun; enormous balls of gas."[7]

The sun is a ball of gas made up mostly of the light-weight elements: hydrogen and helium. And so are all the other stars we see in the night sky.

The earth, on the other hand, is abounding with heavy complex elements and all kinds of molecular compounds. In the vast universe, this is a rare sight. According to Dr. Fred Hoyle, professor at England's Cambridge University:

> "Aside from hydrogen and helium (the light-weight elements), there are practically no other elements in the universe. In the case of our sun, heavier elements make up no more than a single percent...."

> "Celestial bodies such as nebulae and most of the stars," he continues, "are made up of the same substance as our sun. It is very different from the substance of the earth. So it is important to know that, cosmically speaking, the room that you are in right now is an extremely unusual substance. And you, yourself, are also an extremely unusual being."*[8]

Earth is also special in terms of its beauty. Astronauts say that Earth seen from outer space is more beautiful than any photograph could ever depict. An American astronaut who has been to the moon says:

"Seeing the earth from outer space is an awe inspiring experience. There is no way such beauty could have ever come into existence by accident. It is absolutely unthinkable that some day at some time, the elementary particles accidentally bumped into each other, combined, and ended up like this."

"Cosmically speaking, the room that you are in right now is an extremely unusual substance. And you, yourself, are also an extremely unusual being."

"The earth is that beautiful, and seeing the earth from outer space convinces you that it couldn't possibly have taken shape entirely by accident, without plan or purpose. It's not logical. I wish I could show it to someone; I almost feel selfish being one of the handful who's seen it."[9]

He is a man who has actually seen the earth from outer space. And he was certainly impressed by its beauty. Perhaps it is because the earth was specially designed to be lived on that it is so beautiful. Biophysicist Frank Allen comments:

"On Earth, the conditions suitable for maintaining life are so numerous that it cannot be assumed to be the product of accident."*

The earth does have a lot of conditions that are suitable for maintaining life—enough to make you think that it was indeed, specially designed to be a place with life—especially human life. Earth is exactly what the astronauts call it: "the oasis of the universe."

9. Sun and Stars: Made on the Same Day

ACCORDING TO the Bible, the sun we see in the day sky and the stars we see in the night sky were all made on the fourth day of creation (see Genesis 1:16). It is important that the Bible states that the sun and the stars were made on the very same day, and does not state that the sun is special.

The people of older times used to put the sun in a completely different category from the stars in the night sky. They used to worship the sun. But the Bible does not put the sun in any different category than the stars.

Scientists say that the stars (fixed stars) we see in the night sky are just like the sun we see in the day sky. All the stars we see in the night sky, except for Venus and Mars and other planets of our solar system, are called "fixed stars." They are all simple colossal bodies of hydrogen and helium just like the sun.

Fixed stars are the same as the sun. They are suns, and the sun of our solar system is one of them. There is no difference between them. It is reasonable that the Bible states that the sun and the stars were made on the very same day.

10. The Galaxy's Only Intelligent Beings

EVEN THOUGH all the stars in the night sky are radiant bodies of gas that cannot maintain life, a lot of people say:

"Well, I'm sure there are other solar systems here and there in this vast universe. And there must be other planets there with life just like Earth, too." But lately, some astronomers associations have come forth declaring:

"There are no other civilizations in the entire galaxy!"

For example, in 1975, when scientists were busy scanning the skies and trying to make radio-wave contact with possible extraterrestrial civilizations, Dr. Michael Hart, professor at America's Trinity University, aroused the international "Fact 'A' Controversy."

He had released a thesis propounding that there is no extraterrestrial intelligent life in our galaxy. He later participated in a wide range of activities, including presiding at symposiums entitled "Where are the Extraterrestrials?" at Maryland University.

Using the theory of evolution, in which life materialized by a series of phenomenal flukes over billions of years, as the precept for his hypothetical argument, Dr. Hart concluded:

"The point I'm trying to make is that if there really are a lot of extraterrestrial civilizations, some of them would have already accomplished what we are still only dreaming of doing when circumstances permit—starship travel; space exploration missions; and space colonization.

"Not only should the extraterrestrials have been spotted by now," he continues, "they would have colonized the earth and the rest of the solar system ages ago. If a lot of life forms really do exist in the galaxy, by now, they would have had more than ample time to develop into technologically advanced societies, send out space exploration teams, and colonize other planets. (From the point of view of the evolution theory, billions upon billions of years have already passed.) But here on Earth, we haven't even seen them yet. They haven't come here.

"Of course, there are many other angles from which this can be debated. But the way I see it, this plain and simple point is confirmation that there is no other intelligent life in the entire galaxy."[10]

The professor says that for one single cell of a living organism to come into existence, it would take a sequence of coincidences too numerous to be imagined. And that it could never happen twice in one galaxy:

"On a million trillion planets, for a million trillion years, in a million trillion chemical reactions, one little cell might materialize if you're lucky. It would be such a fluke occurrence."[11]

If those are the odds for one little cell to materialize, what would be the odds for a highly developed intelligent being? For a human being to materialize by accident would be virtually in the realm of the impossible.

Therefore, we should consider the thought that "the universe is so vast, there must be other intelligent beings out there somewhere" to be a rash statement. The point I am trying to make of all this is that the existence of human beings and the other life-forms on the earth is an unparalleled phenomenon. The Bible says:

"The highest heavens belong to the Lord, but the earth He has given to man." (Psalm 115:16)

To manifest his infinite greatness, God made the universe boundless. But he made the earth small. The heavens belong to the Lord, and he made the earth "to be inhabited" (Isaiah 45:18). Physically, Earth is not the center of the universe, or of the Milky Way, or even of the solar system for that matter. But it was created to be the most special planet.

Earth, meeting all the requirements to have nurtured life, and to maintain life, is the only planet of its kind in the whole universe. Like a dazzling jewel in the desert, it is a small but precious planet in the vast universe. Physically, the earth might not be so big, and it might not be the center of the universe, but because God "has given the earth to man" (Psalm 115:16), it is the center of his attention.

11. Creation Was Scheduled

THE MOST important thing that the Bible tells us through the narration about creation is that God created the earth and the rest of the universe using a scheduled plan.

In the beginning, God brought the continuum of time, space, and matter into existence. At first, it was in chaos. Then God applied energy to it sorting everything into order, bringing it up to the high-level state that it is in today.

The "first dust" (Proverbs 8:26 NASB) formed the simple, and in turn, the more complex material used to create the celestial bodies.

Furthermore, he made the most basic ingredient for life, the water molecule. For the earth, he had made enough water molecules to form the oceans.

God finished all this in the first half of Day One of creation—everything from the bringing out of the continuum of time and space to the creation of matter containing water.

He also made light on the same day. This light was at the center of what was to become the solar system. It was a pre-sun, or in other words, the material that God later used to form the sun of today. So God divided darkness and light—night and day—on Day One.

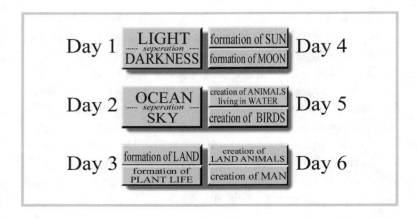

For the rest of the six days of creation, please take a look at the chart. From the chart, we can see that Days One, Two, and Three correspond to Days Four, Five, and Six. Day One is clearly parallel to Day Four; Day Two to Day Five; Day Three to Day Six.

On Day One, the separation of light and darkness—day and night—neatly parallels the events on Day Four: the formation of the sun, which rules the day, and the moon, which rules the night.

On Day Two, the separation of the water above the expanse from the water below it, creating the oceans and the atmosphere of air, parallels the events on Day Five—the creation of the fish and the other animals that live in the water and the birds, of which most fly in the sky.

And on Day Three, the forming of the land parallels the creation of the reptiles, mammals, and other land animals on Day Six. Also, the creation of plant life on Day Three parallels the creation of man on Day Six.

What does this tell us? First of all, it tells us that the earth and the rest of the universe were created with a scheduled plan. And that it was a great being with intelligence who designed it.

Secondly, we can see the separate-and-then-develop process that God used: the separation of light and darkness; the separation of land, ocean, and sky; and then the creation of the various kinds of life. A readily comprehensible example of this separate-and-then-develop process can be seen in the embryonic development in the womb of a pregnant woman.

At first a single egg cell divides into two cells, which in turn, continue dividing and multiplying into a conglomeration of cells. This develops into an embryo, fetus, and eventually into a life-form with high-level functions. The same separate-and-then-develop process was used in the creation of the earth and the rest of the universe.

Another thing that the narration about creation tells us is this: in the whole universe, God created man last.

When parents are expecting a baby, they get the diapers, crib, baby clothes, toys, and all the other necessary things ready in advance, and then wait for the baby to be born. In the same way, God prepared the earth and the rest of the universe in advance, and then brought man into it.

12. Creation of Universe by Superb Intelligence

THE WORD "universe" first appears in Chinese writings of the Han period (the second century B.C.), which explain the word by reference to the Chinese characters for "time" and "space"; i.e., the "universe" refers to all of time and space.

Since the days of Einstein, physics has regarded time and space as being one and the same in so-called "space-time," the universe being a continuum of space and time. When we speak of the "universe," it refers to space-time and all that exists within the continuum, including the galaxy, stars, sun, and earth.

The universe refers to everything in existence. Thus, there is only one universe, although scientists recently argue that there may be several more. They propose that there is another or even several other than our universe. Of course, even assuming that there may be other universes in existence, we cannot easily move from our universe to another one, nor can we really understand much about other such universes.

I am not saying that other universes do actually exist, but in order to better understand our universe, let us imagine for a moment that there are in fact two universes.

One of these contains galaxy, sun, and planets, but there are no human beings or indeed any life in existence. It is a material world only. The other universe is the universe in which we now live. In that universe exists the intelligent life-form of human beings. Now, there is no doubt that both of these can be called a universe, but the meaning of existence in each universe is completely different.

In the universe which we inhabit, human beings are aware of the existence and nature of the universe through means of intellectual research. Astronomers study the stars, theoretical physicists consider the origin of the universe, and engineers send rockets into space to explore the stars. Human beings are, in other words, involved in the universe in a variety of ways.

Conversely, in the universe containing no intelligent life, nobody is aware of its existence. The fact that it will never be recognized by anyone means that it is practically nothing. No matter how expansive and how beautiful that universe may be, nobody can ever appreciate its existence or its nature, which renders it "next to non-existent."

It is, practically speaking, nothing. If "awareness," is our standard, then a universe without intelligent life is "a universe without existence," even if it does, in fact, exist. On the other hand, a universe like ours, which has intelligent life, is a universe which exists.

13. The Existence of the Universe in Superb Balance

THIS MATTER has now become one of considerable controversy among scientists.

You have undoubtedly thought about this kind of thing as well. Why didn't the universe in which we live become just a material universe, rather than one which is inhabited by intelligent life?

Recently scientists have begun to think that the universe was already "programmed" at the time of its birth to become a universe bearing intelligent life.

This fact can be seen, for example, in the "fundamental physical constants."

According to Assistant Professor Takuya Matsuda of Kyoto University, in our universe there are certain "fixed numerical values" of, for example, the speed of light, electron mass, gravity constant, and Planck constant. Such numerical values appear so masterfully controlled that one can only conclude they "were chosen as prerequisites for the generation of intelligent life."

For example, we know that the speed of light is 300,000 kilometers (187,500 miles) per second. However, let us assume for a moment that the speed of light in today's universe is minutely different from that speed. Even such a small variation would mean that human beings could never exist. At first glance, the speed of light and intelligent life appear to have no relationship, but in fact they are closely connected. The human body is largely composed of protein, and a large part of protein is made up of carbon.

The reason why carbon atoms are able to efficiently create highly polymerized compounds like protein is because the energy of a carbon atom in the sense of quantum mechanics has just the right numerical value. One thing which regulates the energy value is the speed of light, or the gravity constant or the Planck constant.

In other words, in the ordered system of the universe today, if the speed of light were not 300,000 kilometers per second, then carbon atoms could not maintain the energy value, and consequently organic compounds such as protein could not be formed, with the end result being that life could not be generated. Thus, even if another universe exists with a speed of light that is 30,000 kilometers per second or 3000 kilometers per second, such a universe would not be "inhabited by intelligent life."

However, in our universe, the value of the speed of light is just right, which is why our universe contains "intelligent life" and why we are now thinking about "why there is a universe."

Further, according to Professor Humitaka Satoh of Kyoto University, human beings could also not exist if, for example, the mass of electrons were varied by just 1 percent. You are probably tempted to think that just 1 percent variation in weight would not make such a big difference, but, in fact, even 1 percent would lead to this result. This shows the extent to which the universe is masterfully controlled to produce "intelligent life."

14. Universe Programmed for Inhabitation by Intelligent Life

The American scientist Dr. Carter contends that not only life, but also stars and the galaxy owe their existence to the fact that the fundamental physical constants have just the right numerical values.

The "genius scientist in a wheelchair," Dr. Stephen W. Hawking, also states that the form of our universe today is due to the fact that fundamental physical constants have just the right numerical values. If the physical constants were different, the universe would probably have either self-destructed soon after its birth, or, conversely, developed at an alarming pace.

There may be or have been other universes, but there certainly has never been a "universe inhabited by intelligent life." It is not an overstatement to claim that the universe in which we live—the universe inhabited by intelligent life—was internally programmed from the start to support intelligent life.

Let us consider, by way of analogy, a technician who builds a television. He decides what the numerical value should be in order to fix the voltage of the Braun tube. He fixes the sound emission according to a certain numerical value. He produces a television by determining the various numerical values in relation to the voltage and current of each component of the television.

The television will not function if he makes a mistake with even one of those numerical values: there will be no picture, or strange noises will come out of it, making it fit only for the trash heap.

In the same way, the existence of our marvelous universe as a "universe inhabited by intelligent life " is due to God's ordaining the most appropriate fundamental physical values in relation to each aspect of the material world.

Producing just one television set has required the skills of many intelligent human beings, long years of research, and much effort. This being so, imagine then, what a profoundly great intelligence must have created the human being's highly complex form of life as well as the vast universe. Israel's King David once sang:

> "How many are your works, O Lord! In wisdom you made them all; the earth is full of your creatures." (Psalm 104:24)

And again,

"Give thanks to the Lord, …To Him who made
the heavens with skill." (Psalm 136:1,5 NASB)

We too, when we consider the creation of the universe
in such superb balance, cannot help but join King David in
praise of the wisdom of God, the Creator. God, whose intelligence is far vaster than human intelligence, created a universe
inhabited by intelligent life-forms.

15. First and Second Laws of Thermodynamics Reveal Creation of the Universe

IN PHYSICS, there is something called the "First Law of
Thermodynamics" and the "Second Law of Thermodynamics."
Taking these two scientific laws together, the fact of creation of
the universe can be clearly understood.

The first law of thermodynamics is known as the "Law
of Energy Conservation," while the second law of thermodynamics is known as the "Law of Energy Decay (Entropy)."
According to Hitoshi Takeuchi, Professor Emeritus of Tokyo
University, the first and second laws of thermodynamics are
in fact what today's physical science confirms to be the only
"absolute scientific truth."

Other scientific laws, whether they be Newton's laws of
motion, Einstein's theory of relativity or the principles of
quantum physics which have been developed in the twentieth
century, are nothing more than "tentative truths," or, in other
words, hypotheses.

However, the law of energy conservation and the law of
energy decay (entropy) have been proven by repeated experimental tests and are regarded as indisputable scientific truths.
These laws form the basis of scientific thought and are
absolute scientific truths controlling the whole universe.

Considered together, these two laws reveal that a great supernatural force created the universe. Let us first look at the law of energy conservation.

(1) The first law of thermodynamics describes the absence of change in total energy volume before and after physical or chemical reaction. It is not possible to destroy energy itself, nor is it possible to create it anew. Energy changes in form only and not in quantity. Therefore, energy can never be generated spontaneously. And energy also contains mass. This is referred to as the "equivalence of mass and energy," such that mass is also regarded as one form of energy.

So we know that the universe possesses certain energy-containing mass. Therefore, from the law of energy conservation, which asserts that energy cannot be spontaneously generated, we can conclude that the universe could never have developed by itself. In other words, the universe was not born from natural forces.

(2) Next, let us look at the meaning of the law of energy decay (entropy). Entropy is the measure of the quantity of energy which is not capable of use. The inevitable increase over time of the entropy, that is, the decay of the energy capable of use is called the law of energy decay.

Simply stated, this law is consistent with the proverb "It's no use crying over spilt milk." In other words, the more one uses energy, the more that energy is altered to energy of a lesser quality such that, over time, it cannot ultimately be converted into use.

Over time, all physical and chemical reactions move in the direction of order to chaos, from a state of abundant available energy to a state of largely non-available energy. With the passage of time, it becomes much more difficult for physical or chemical reactions to occur. In other words, entropy of the universe—the measure of energy in the universe not able to be utilized—is increasing over time.

It is scientifically recognized that, as considerable time passes (several billions of years), the universe will at some stage eventually reach a stage of "heat death," at which point physical and chemical reactions cease to occur.

"Heat death" does not mean death due to heat, but rather a state of death of the universe in the thermodynamic sense. The amount of non-available energy increases to a stage that no reactions occur and, in effect, the universe "dies."

But the fact that today's universe has not yet reached this state of "heat death" implies that the universe does not have a limitless age. Accordingly, the universe must have had a beginning. The universe has not existed since some eternally distant past.

It must have commenced within limited time at some ascertainable point in the past. At the time of such birth of the universe, there was minimum entropy. But entropy of the universe is gradually increasing over time. And the universe is now on the way to "heat death."

So what conclusion can we draw by combining (1) and (2) above? We learn from (2) that the world had a "beginning," and it is evident from (1) that such beginning did not occur spontaneously. So some great supernatural force can only have especially created the universe. That great creator is the "God" referred to in the Bible:

"In the beginning God created the heavens and the earth" (Genesis 1:1).

The first and second laws of thermodynamics verify the truth of these Biblical words.

CHAPTER THREE

✦

Sudden Environmental Change Due to the Great Flood

1. There Really Was the Great Flood of Noah

NUCLEONICS PROFESSOR at the Virginia Institute of Technology in the U.S.A., Dr. Whitelaw, has presented impressive evidence which reveals that at one time in the history of the world there occurred a widespread decrease in the number of living things.[1]

Professor Whitelaw collected fossils of living creatures amounting to fifteen thousand or so, and determined the age in which they existed according to the carbon-14 dating method. This C-14 method is one method of date estimation by radioactive isotopes, and is widely used to estimate the age of living creatures.

Professor Whitelaw discovered from this study that, for the sample dating back to the period between 3500–4000 B.C.

there was a sudden decrease in the number of living things such as human beings, animals, and trees.

He commented, however, with regard to this dramatic diminishing of living things, that he thought the results of this survey yielded dates slightly older than the actual dates and that, in fact, the age in which such sudden decrease occurred was about the time of Noah's Great Flood (according to the Bible, Noah's Flood took place around 2500 B.C.).

Professor Whitelaw describes how, after the decrease, the number of living things gradually increased until, with respect to animals and human beings, it regained the original number around the time of Christ. With regard to trees, the number has gradually increased but has not yet regained the original number.

Assuming that in the history of the world there was in fact a dramatic decrease in the number of living things populating the earth, there can be no doubt that it was due to the occurrence on the earth at that time of a great "natural catastrophe" or great cataclysm.

It is intriguing that this concurs with the Bible's account of Noah's Flood. According to the Bible, the majority of human beings and land dwelling creatures were wiped out by the Flood. Also, it can be assumed that many ocean-dwelling creatures were swallowed up and drowned by the swelling waters of such a flood.

Was there really a Great Flood in Noah's time? Many people believe it to be a myth or a fairy tale. However, more recently an increasing number of scientists reason that acknowledgement of a cataclysmic change in the past goes a long way in helping to explain the various scientific evidence relating to the history of the earth.

Not only the Bible has recorded this legend that the earth was once swallowed up by an enormous flood; it is known to Babylonians, Assyrians, Egyptians, Persians, Hindus, Greeks,

Evidence of the Great Flood in the time of Noah is discovered at places of all over the world.

Chinese, Phrygians, Fiji Islanders, Eskimos, Aboriginal Americans, Indians, Brazilians, Peruvians, and indeed every branch of the whole human race.[2]

The legend of the Great Flood can be found among Semitic languages, Aryan (Indo-European) languages, as well as Turanian languages. The book *Earth as The Target* comments:

> "Since, in the everyday experience of man, a flood is not a large-scale event and does not happen everywhere, it is unusual to create a tale of an irresistible Great Flood which can wipe out everything in its path.... So why is the legend of such a flood common to all races of mankind? Why does such a legend exist even among races living in dry lands at the peaks of mountains far from coastal regions, such as Central Mexico and Central Asia?"*

Moreover, although they differ in certain details, many of the legends of the Great Flood, as they have been passed down over time, are consistent in their assertion that all mankind except for one family was destroyed by the Great Flood.[3]

The fact of this universal legend of the Great Flood can only be understood by the idea that, when the surviving members of Noah's family began to repopulate the earth and the numbers of mankind increased, the record of the Great Flood's actual occurrence in bygone days was passed on as a legend among all races of mankind.

The universality of this legend should be seen not as a product of the imagination of each race in the world, but as a record of an actual event in history which has been conveyed from one generation to the next.

In view of this, the numbers of intellectuals who are recently coming to recognize the reality of Noah's Flood are increasing. For example, the October 4, 1975 issue of *Science News* magazine concludes, after examining the various evidences relating to the Great Flood, that these confirm "there was a giant flood encompassing the entire earth."*

Additionally, Highness Mikasa, a member of the Imperial family of Japan, who is known as an archaeologist, comments in his book:

> "Did the Great Flood actually ever occur in fact? The results of excavations in recent years by archaeologists provide excellent proof that such a flood did actually occur."

2. A Worldwide Flood!?

ONE POINT which often poses a problem is the question of whether the Great Flood was a regional flood confined to the basin of the Tigris-Euphrates river, or whether it was a flood over all of the earth.

Those who assert it was a regional flood claim that the occurrence of a major flood of a kind which would have covered all of the mountain peaks of the whole earth is impossible. Where would such a massive volume of water have come from and where did it go?

I will show that the idea of the Great Flood having been on a worldwide scale better explains various scientific evidences. The signs of the Great Flood have been revealed all over the world. Let us look a little later at the question of how it was possible for the flood to cover the entire surface of the earth.

The Holy Bible, too, does not describe the Great Flood as having been confined to a particular region. If the Great Flood was in fact a regional one, there would have been no necessity for Noah to build an ark. He could merely have moved to an area beyond the reaches of the flood.

3. Pre-Flood Water Vapor Canopy

IF WE acknowledge that in the past there was in fact a worldwide flood as recorded in the Bible then, as we will now discover, many of the matters in the history of the world which have been dismissed as an enigma, can be clearly understood. These matters are the pillars of "scientific creationism" (creation science) which is the viewpoint represented in this book.

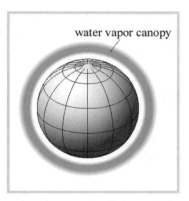

water vapor canopy

Scientific creationism is the theory that the various scientific evidences available to us concerning the birth of life and the world can be better explained, not by evolutionary processes, but by the idea that these were individually and originally created.

Before the Great Flood, there was the water vapor canopy called "water above the expanse (sky)" (Genesis 1:7) above the earth's atmosphere.

According to scientific creationism, the world was created pursuant to a plan, and each variety of living creatures was originally created and appeared "according to their various kinds" (Genesis 1:11). Those who adopt this view are creationists, and their number is gradually increasing among scientists and intellectuals.

First, let us look at the matter of where the Great Flood came from. Do creationists consider the question of how the Great Flood came about? According to Genesis 1:7, before the Great Flood there was water above the earth's atmosphere called "water above the expanse (sky)."

In relation to the "water above the expanse," Dr. Henry M. Morris, a professor of Hydraulics at Minnesota University in the U.S., says:

> "It could not have been the clouds of water droplets which now float in the atmosphere, because the Scripture says it was 'above the sky.'

> "The 'water above the expanse' thus probably constituted a vast blanket of water vapor above…in the high-temperature region…and extending far into space."[4]

Thus, scientists who stand by this creationist theory think that, before the Great Flood, there was a "vast blanket of water vapor" or "water vapor canopy" in the upper atmosphere. The Bible calls it "the water above the expanse" (Genesis 1:7).

As everybody knows, in today's atmosphere, when you climb a high mountain, the temperature decreases as the altitude rises. This is only up to about the height of 10 kilometers (6 miles), but, conversely, at a distance of about 130 kilometers (81 miles) from the earth's surface, the temperature becomes extremely high, reaching 100 degrees Celsius (212°F), and in some cases more than 1000°C (1832°F).

Such a high temperature zone exists in the upper atmosphere. Even at a distance of about 50 kilometers (31 miles) into the upper atmosphere, the temperature is relatively high, due to the heat given off by ozone.

Before the Great Flood, the water vapor canopy above the sky pressed the atmosphere below it, so the air pressure on the surface of the earth at that time was higher than today's. It also made the atmosphere structure different from the current one.

Then, before the Great Flood, what was the atmosphere structure like?

The sunlight in those days reached to the surface of the earth abundantly as it does today. For many people, the expression "water vapor" no doubt conjures up an image of "something white" like steam rising from a boiling kettle.

However, such steam is in fact minute water droplets which were formed after water vapor was released into the air and cooled down, whereas "water vapor" itself is colorless, transparent, and invisible to the naked eye. The water vapor canopy in the upper atmosphere was also transparent so that rays of sunlight poured brightly down on the people on the earth.

The sun radiates not only visible rays but also ultraviolet rays, infrared rays, and other rays of various wavelengths. Water vapor lets visible rays pass through well, but absorbs infrared rays, which are electromagnetic waves having power to warm up as you look at an infrared ray stove.

So, the water vapor canopy in the upper part of the atmosphere was absorbing the infrared rays and was being warmed up.

Water vapor does not absorb ultraviolet rays well. They passed through the water vapor canopy and formed under it or in the middle part of the atmosphere a layer of ozone, which is formed by combining oxygen molecules in the air with oxygen atoms produced by the dissociation effect of ultraviolet rays from the sun. In that process it produced heat, and the heat was warming up the atmosphere nearby.

Ozone can be formed near the surface of the earth if there are ultraviolet rays and oxygen, but even when formed, it would decompose at once by dust in the air, etc., thus the density of ozone near the surface of the earth becomes very low.

In other words, a layer of ozone is formed in the upper sky. As I will mention later, before the Great Flood the density of oxygen was higher than today's; there was plenty of oxygen extending to the upper sky. Thus, by the heat produced in the ozone layer, the water vapor canopy above it was kept at a high temperature and in the state of water vapor.

Water vapor is actually lighter in weight than air. So, it is not at all illogical to reason from the standpoint of physics, that in the high temperature zone of the upper atmosphere there was once an enormous amount of water vapor. It was this water vapor canopy which fell down over the earth and became the flooding rains pouring down "forty days and forty nights" in the days of Noah.

4. Earth's Temperate Climate Before the Great Flood

THE LAYER of water vapor covered the earth's upper atmosphere like a canopy, making the whole surface of the earth temperate, just as if it were inside a greenhouse. Dr. Seikou Tsukioka, an instructor at Yamagata University of Japan, says:

> "Up until then, there were very few 'ups and downs' of the earth and it was covered by a thick layer of water vapor (the water above the expanse). Because of this, the whole earth was temperate all year

round, just like inside a greenhouse. The fact that trees from ancient times have no growth rings is proof that there were no extremes of hot and cold and an even temperature throughout the year."[5]

In addition, the fact that coral fossils can be found in the vicinity of the South and North Poles provides further evidence that the whole earth was once temperate. This is because coral cannot grow except in water temperatures of 20°C (68°F) or more.

There is a "never-ending layer of coal"[6] in the Antarctic continent which is exposed in some places, and a layer of coal has also been found in the Arctic Circle. As coal is formed from the decomposed remains of plants, this also speaks eloquently of the fact that both of these now extremely cold areas were once temperate zones in which flora thrived.

The remains of creatures which can currently exist only in warm areas are being found in places all over the world. In fact, the remains of dinosaurs, which are thought to have required a temperate climate, as well as other cold-blooded animals, can be found all over the world. A French scholar has said:

There is a "never-ending layer of coal" exposed in some places in the Antarctic continent.

"Notwithstanding latitudinal extremes, the earth's climate was once predominately humid and temperate...Ceaselessly growing giant trees covered both islands and continents...At that time, there was little variation in temperatures from summer

The earth's climate was once predominately humid and temperate.

to winter. At a northern latitude of 70 degrees in Greenland, fig trees have been unearthed, and in Siberia, hemp palms have been excavated."[7]

As this describes, at one stage in the earth's past, the whole earth was temperate with very little temperature change from summer to winter. There can be no doubt that the atmosphere then was different from today's. There was a strong "greenhouse effect." The water vapor canopy in the earth's upper atmosphere explains it most precisely.

5. No Rainbows Prior to the Great Flood

BEFORE THE Great Flood, there was no great temperature difference between polar and equatorial regions, owing to the canopy of water vapor. All regions were moderately warm.

The Bible says that in the Eden period, "God had not sent rain," but the land obtained sufficient moisture because "streams came up from the earth and watered the whole surface of the ground" (Genesis 2:5-6). The word translated as "streams" here means "groundwater" in Hebrew. There was much groundwater in those days, and it formed numerous streams here and there on earth. These streams formed rivers (Genesis 2:10).

And after the Eden period, prior to the great flood, the air and the land would have been sufficiently moistened by the evaporation of water, mist and probably rainfall. Plants and animals on the earth obtained a comfortable humidity. But even if there was rainfall, no "rainbows" could be observed from the earth, for the atmospheric pressure condition before the Great Flood was different from that of today.

Rainbows can be seen after rainfall today because droplets of water floating in the air, when struck by rays of light from the sun, become like a prism which refracts the sun's light. Since the refraction rate varies with the colors of light, a total of seven colors can be observed.

However, even in the present-day atmosphere, rainbows cannot be seen in the middle of the day, when the elevation of the sun reaches 42 degrees or more. At such elevation, refracted light does not reach the earth's surface.

Whether or not light is refracted by drops of water and the rate of such refraction depend on the density difference between drops of water and the air.

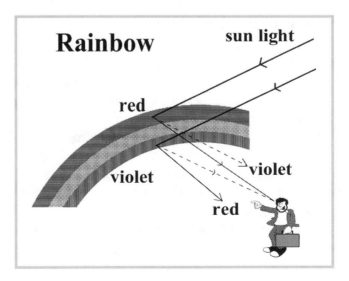

As I will mention later, the atmospheric pressure in the period prior to the Great Flood was about double the level of today. So during that period, the difference in density of the air and of water droplets would not have been as great as today. Accordingly, since there would have been no refraction of light necessary to create a rainbow effect, rainbows could not have been observed during those times.

The Bible states, in Genesis 9:11-13, that rainbows were able to be seen after the Great Flood, and are a sign of God's covenant that "never again will all life be cut off by the waters of a flood…" So, before that, no rainbow was seen.

Not only this, it is thought that the world's climate before the Great Flood was vastly different from that of today. As Dr. Henry M. Morris describes, with respect to the earth's surface before the Great Flood:

> "The combination of warm temperature and adequate moisture everywhere would be conducive later to extensive stands of lush vegetation all over the world, with no barren deserts and ice caps."[8]

6. Paradox of the Dark Sun

UP UNTIL NOW, evolutionists have not been able to sufficiently explain why, in the history of the earth, there was once a time in which the climate was more temperate than today. In fact, this problem has perplexed evolutionists as "the paradox of the dark sun."

The sun shines as it burns up hydrogen, which is thereby transformed into helium. Thus, it is scientifically known that the sun is gradually becoming rich in helium and shines more brightly as a result. With the passage of time, the sun is becoming increasingly "sunnier."

This means that in the past the sun must have been darker than it is today. Professor Carl Sagan estimates that the brightness of the sun around the time of the birth of the earth would have been only about 70 percent of its brightness today.

Accordingly, if we assume that the earth's atmospheric conditions have always been about the same as today, then it stands to reason that the earth must have once been colder. However, this conclusion clearly contradicts the well-known geological evidence that the earth was once much warmer than today. This is called the "dark sun paradox."

In this connection, Dr. Takafumi Matsui, of Tokyo University, comments, "This kind of thing suggests that in the past, the earth's atmosphere was different to today."[9] In other words, the only possible explanation for the fact that the earth was once temperate is to reason that the atmospheric conditions were once different from those of the present day.

This is one reason why creationists assert that there was once a "water vapor canopy in the upper atmosphere," which offers an extremely sound explanation why there was a temperate period in the earth's history.

How was the water vapor canopy formed? As I earlier mentioned in chapter 1, when the earth was born through the collision of asteroids, the atmosphere created was a "water vapor atmosphere."[10] This "water vapor atmosphere" later cooled down to become torrential rain, forming an expansive ocean over the surface of the earth.

However, according to the Bible, not all of the water vapor making up the water vapor atmosphere became rain, which eventually formed the ocean. It is written that,

"God said 'Let there be an expanse between the waters (water vapor atmosphere) to separate water from water.' So God made the expanse (sky) and separated the water under the expanse (ocean) from the water above it (water vapor canopy)." (Genesis 1:6,7)

In other words, not the entire water vapor atmosphere which initially existed was completely transformed into ocean. Part of it remained to form the water vapor canopy in the uppermost layer called the "water above the expanse," with the atmosphere (expanse) below it, and the ocean further below.

In this way, it is thought, the "water above the expanse" (water vapor canopy), "expanse" (atmosphere), and "water below the expanse" (ocean) were formed.

(Some people think that "the expanse" means the interstellar space and "the water above the expanse" exists at cosmic distances away from the earth, billions of light-years away.

However, there is no evidence that there exists or existed such water far away from the earth. And this thought cannot explain appropriately how the worldwide rain for forty days and forty nights came.

As I will mention later, the thought that "the expanse" means the atmosphere (sky) and "the water above the expanse" means the water vapor canopy above the atmosphere can explain various scientific facts appropriately.)

7. Formation of Mountains and Valleys by the Great Flood

EVEN ADMITTING the existence of the water vapor canopy described above, you may still be wondering how that led to a flood so great as to cover even the tops of mountains all over the world. But in fact, it is not essential to this idea of a "worldwide flood" that there has been such a massive volume of water as to cover mountains existing today, such as Mt. Everest.

It is generally thought that, before the time of Noah's Flood, the surface of the earth was not as uneven as today. Before the Great Flood, the earth's surface was much more even than the present day. *Scientific Monthly* reports, with respect to the past earth, "in terms of climate and natural conditions, there would have been no obstructive high mountains."

Before the Flood, the face of the earth was much more level than the surface of today's earth.

There is abundant evidence for the proposition that the earth's surface has undergone huge changes up to the present day. Even in more recent years, the highs and lows of the earth's surface have changed significantly. In 1950, for example, the strong earthquake which hit the Assam area in India caused major changes to the mountain valleys of the eastern section of the Himalayan range.

What about the bottom of the ocean? Today, many mountains are being discovered at the bottom of the ocean which are thought to have once been above sea level before sinking to their current positions. Additionally, coral reefs, which can be formed only in shallow waters, are being found over a vast area of the deep ocean floor, revealing that they were submerged in identical fashion over a wide expanse of the bottom of the ocean.

Thus, the question as to how the Great Flood came to cover the whole earth can be explained as follows: Before the Flood, the face of the earth was much more level than the surface of today's earth.

The "water above the expanse" fell to earth as rain. The amount of rainfall at that time is estimated by Dr. Dillow to have been about 12 meters (39 feet). Thus, even assuming the level nature of the earth's surface, this amount would surely not have been enough to completely cover the earth. However, the Bible records:

> "The waters flooded the earth for a hundred and fifty days." (Genesis 7:24)

Thus, even after the rain fell over "forty days and forty nights," the water level continued to rise. The word translated here "flood," in the original Hebrew *gabar*, is translated in other verses "rise." In Genesis 7:18, it is translated "The waters rose and increased greatly on the earth." Also in Genesis 7:20, "The waters rose and covered the mountains to a depth of more than twenty feet."

The water level continued to rise for 150 days, even after the rain for 40 days stopped. This was because the floodwaters which were swept over the earth by the rapid currents caused enormous changes to the earth's crust.

According to the Bible, there was abundant "water below the earth" before the Great Flood. For example, it is recorded that huge amounts of water sprang from the ground in the Garden of Eden. (The original language translated as "streams" in Genesis 2:6 means "water below the earth.") That water was divided to form four rivers.

This kind of groundwater must have existed all over the earth before the Great Flood. The tectonic movements occasioned by the floodwaters brought about the release all over the earth of these massive amounts of groundwater. Simultaneously, the crustal movements must have caused upheaval of the ocean floor and a rise in sea level.

In fact, the Bible tells us that when the Great Flood began:

> "the mountains rose; the valleys sank down…"
> (Psalm 104:8 NASB)

This reveals that enormous crustal movement took place. Beginning with deep sections of the ocean, these movements must have led to the formation of mountain ranges on the ocean floor.

It is well known that mountain-forming crustal movements occur more easily in the ocean. As a result of this, the surface ocean level rose, and what began as heavy rain soon turned into a worldwide flood, covering all the mountains over the entire surface of the earth.

Then, after 150 days "the water receded steadily…" (Genesis 8:3). This was because around that time, in all regions of the world, mountains had risen up and valleys had become submerged. The undulations of the earth's surface became much more extreme and water settled in the lower regions, with areas left above the water becoming land.

The Great Flood also caused the formation of massive valleys such as the Japan Deep, as well as great mountain ranges such as the Rocky Mountains, the Andes, and the

When the Great Flood began, "the mountains rose; the valleys sank down…" (Psalm 104:8 NASB)

Himalayas. It is well-known that these high mountain ranges were formed relatively recently.

Additionally, rocks at the peaks of tall mountains such as Mt. Everest are aqueous rocks which have often been found to contain fossils of marine life. The most reasonable explanation for this is the idea that the mass of earth which sunk below the surface of the water as a result of the Great Flood later rose up to form these high mountains.

According to geophysicists, if we were to level all of the undulations on the earth's surface today so as to make it even, all areas of the world would sink about 2400 meters (7900 feet) below sea level. Thus, it is only the earth's undulations which keep the whole world from becoming completely submerged in water.

8. Why Pre-Flood Mankind Had Long Life Span

ACCORDING TO the Bible, human beings living before the Great Flood had an extremely long life span. An examination of the age of the people living before the Great Flood, as recorded in the family tree of Adam in chapter 5 of Genesis, reveals that most people lived to be around 900 years old.

The reason why people living before the Great Flood had such long life spans must have been because it was before the time when God ordained that man should live for a maximum of only "120 years." Genesis 6:3 records:

> "My spirit shall not abide in man for ever, for he
> is flesh, but his days shall be a hundred and twenty
> years." (RSV)

Thus, following the Great Flood, the life span of man gradually became shorter and shorter down to 120 years within several generations, so that modern man can now live no longer than 120 years or so.

Physically speaking, the existence before the Great Flood of the water vapor canopy in the upper atmosphere (the water above the expanse) played a part in the long life span of mankind.

As is commonly known, harmful radioactive rays called "cosmic rays" rain down on the earth continuously both night and day. These are atomic particles which fly to earth at great speed from the far off Milky Way, little noticed but causing significant radioactive damage to human cells.

The following anecdote tells us something about the exact nature of "cosmic rays." An *Apollo* astronaut was flying in a rocket in space. He closed his eyes to sleep but saw an instant flash of bright light. When he asked his fellow astronauts about it, they claimed not to have seen the light. The same thing happened on a different occasion to another astronaut. This phenomenon was later explained as the effects of cosmic rays.

Cosmic rays penetrated through the walls of the spaceship, weaving their path between atoms, but by chance they hit and ionized the atom of an eye nerve cell, thereby causing the flash of light.

In this way, the overflowing cosmic rays from space have an enormous impact on the bodies of living things exposed to them for long periods. However, before the Great Flood, the water vapor canopy acted as a filter of these cosmic rays, such that the number of cosmic rays reaching earth at that time was far less than the present day. The fact that an environment free of cosmic rays plays a significant role in the prolongation of life has been clearly evidenced by recent medical research.

So, the presence of the water vapor canopy protected man from the harmful influences of not only cosmic rays, but also other radiation from the earth's outer spheres, such as ultraviolet rays and x-rays, thereby creating an extremely comfortable environment for living things.

Additionally, the water vapor canopy which was originally exposed to matter such as "solar wind" (the radioactive particles flying away from the sun), when it fell to earth as rain at the time of Noah's Flood, must have caused the quality of water in the ocean, rivers, and underground to suffer change to some greater or lesser degree. It is well known that the quality of an area's water has a tremendous influence on human life span.

The life span of human beings ebbs and flows, depending quite substantially on the quality of the environment. It is quite reasonable to suppose that the dramatic changes to the quality of man's living environment which were brought about after the Great Flood have shortened man's life span.

9. Water Vapor Canopy Becomes Torrential Rain

THE BIBLE records, with respect to the time when the water vapor canopy (the water above the expanse) poured down to earth as floodwaters for forty days and forty nights in the days of Noah, that:

> "…all the springs of the great deep burst forth,
> and the floodgates of the heavens were opened.
> And rain fell on the earth forty days and forty
> nights." (Genesis 7:11,12)

This is how the "water above the expanse" came to fall as heavy rains upon the earth. But how did the water vapor canopy, which until then had been stable in the upper atmosphere, suddenly open its "floodgates" and fall down to earth as rain? The Bible does not mention anything about this. However, there must have been something which happened to upset the balance and stability of the water vapor canopy. Is there any proof regarding this matter?

In 1977, a group of scientists at California University conducted a survey of "cosmic dust" (the dust regularly falling to earth from space) found in the earth's crust. They discovered a very curious thing. Iridium, which is not found in most substances on the earth, was selected as an indicator of cosmic dust.

The amount of cosmic dust which falls to the earth at any given time is practically constant. The amount of iridium which was detected in the vicinity of a layer of fossilized remains, hinting at the sudden death of living creatures such as dinosaurs, ammonites, reptiles, and plankton alike, was not the expected standard amount but thirty times higher.

A layer of iridium was distributed over the whole world. It can only be imagined that a massive "something" came to earth, and at around the same time a major disaster befell the earth, causing the extinction of most living creatures.[11]

One scientist imagines that this "massive something" was in fact an asteroid with a diameter of about 10 kilometers (6 miles). If such a heavenly body collided with earth, its effects would not be limited to just the creation of a large crater on the earth's surface.

Around the point of impact, there would be major earthquakes and fires, as well as ocean tidal waves. Additionally, large amounts of dust and soot would be blown high into the air, reach the upper atmosphere, and spread all over the earth, undoubtedly disrupting the balance of the water vapor canopy.[12]

Other scientists reason that the thing which flew to earth was a comet, which, apart from its nucleus, is composed almost entirely of ice. Dr. Kite, professor of California University, reasons that when the comet approached the earth, it broke apart, causing frozen rain to fall to earth. This would definitely cause a cooling down of the water vapor canopy, triggering the fall of heavy rain.[13]

In any case, no matter what came to the earth, the disaster might have caused the eruption of many volcanoes including submarine volcanoes and release of much underground water vapor or groundwater. Thus:

> "…all the springs of the great deep burst forth,
> and the floodgates of the heavens were opened."
> (Genesis 7:11)

A series of studies have made clear one important fact. In earth's history there occurred a sudden, major worldwide disaster, which triggered the extinction of virtually all living things. World authorities on space science, Michael Allaby and James Lovelock, state in their joint book *Why Did Dinosaurs Become Extinct?*:

> "…This very fact firmly indicates…that the mass extinction of plant and animal life was a widespread, completely unexpected phenomenon caused by some transitory event…the effect of nothing less than a catastrophe."[*14]

It is clear from the records contained in fossils that, in the history of the earth, there was once a sudden disappearance of dinosaurs and other living things, and it is most logical to assume that this mass extinction was triggered by some kind of sudden disaster. There should be no doubt that at the heart of such disaster was the Great Flood, as recorded in the Bible.

10. The Great Flood Leads to Short-Term "Ice Age"

CONDITIONS UPON the earth changed dramatically as a result of the Great Flood. As the heavy rain from the water vapor canopy began to fall, the surface temperature of the earth began to decrease, causing it to become chilled. It was as if the earth was a greenhouse which, with its cover removed, lost its "greenhouse effect," causing a sudden major cooling down of particularly the North and South Polar regions, and the creation of ice fields.

At that time, a large number of plants and animals were trapped in the ice. As a creationist scientist describes it:

"High altitude heavy rain took the form of snow and ice, creating giant glaciers in which animals and plants such as mammoths were suddenly ice-bound and froze to death."[15]

In fact, the body of an icebound mammoth found in Siberia speaks of this sudden freezing to death.

It is estimated today that the bodies of about fifty million mammoths are frozen in ice in Siberia, although mammoths did not originally inhabit areas of extreme cold. The skin of mammoths did not contain the oil-secreting glands of animals which live in polar regions.

In the mouths and stomachs of mammoths which have been discovered frozen in ice, green grasses of plants such as buttercups have been found. In this photo, a mammoth child is discovered in ice in Siberia.)

Additionally, in the mouths and stomachs of mammoths which have been discovered frozen in ice, green grasses of plants such as buttercups have been found. In other words, mammoths did not, as asserted by evolutionists, disappear as a result of lack of food brought on by the gradual appearance of glaciers.

Mammoths lived in temperate areas and ate green plants. They were suddenly caught up in the Great Flood and froze to death while they still had grass in their mouths and stomachs. An article entitled "The Enigma of Giant Frozen Creatures" which appeared in the *Saturday Evening Post* magazine, states:

"Most of the North Pole ice fields are covered with a layer of garbage with a thickness of between 1-300 meters (1-1000 feet) or more. This layer is full of various materials, most of which is frozen hard like rocks…. In some cases, it contains a huge mass of bones and the whole bodies of animals…If one were to defrost and extract these animals from among the mishmash and identify them, the names of varieties would surely fill several pages…"

It continues, "The remains of these animals are scattered all over the area…Most of them still appear perfectly fresh and undamaged, and if not completely upright, then at least resting on their knees…

"In the light of our reasoning to date, this is actually a very shocking fact. A huge herd of well-nourished giant creatures grazed peacefully in sunlit grassy fields, leisurely plucking at buttercup flowers in a place so warm that it would be T-shirt weather for us human beings…. These were not animals that lived in areas of extreme cold…

"However, most of them died, without suffering any superficial damage whatsoever, so suddenly that they did not even have time to swallow the food in their mouths, and then were rapidly frozen. The process of freezing was so rapid that many of the cells of these animals are preserved even today…"[*16]

The frozen remains of these animals reveal that the environment did not change slowly and gradually move into an ice age, but rather, that there was a drastic change which brought about the glaciers. These kinds of matters can be explained very clearly by the drastic change which was brought on the "sudden freezing" of Noah's Flood.

As a result of the Great Flood, the polar regions underwent a dramatic decrease in temperature, bringing on a relatively short "ice age," so that many plants and animals were suddenly trapped beneath the ice.

You are probably thinking, "Yes, but haven't there been various ice ages in the earth's history, not just one?"

In fact, ocean investigations reveal "many difficulties," and sharp conflict with the idea that there have been multiple ice ages. In this regard, Michael J. Oard, a meteorologist with the U.S. Weather Bureau, comments:

> "There are strong indications that there was only one ice age…The main characteristics of the till favor one ice age. Pleistocene fossils are rare in glaciated areas, which is mysterious, if there were many interglacials…"[17]

Mammoths did not disappear as a result of lack of food brought on by glaciers. They lived in temperate areas and ate green plants, but were suddenly caught up in the Great Flood and froze to death.

He concluded that there has in fact been only one ice age, which was brought about by the sudden changes resulting from the Great Flood in the days of Noah.

11. Extinction of Dinosaurs Due to Climatic Changes

IN THIS WAY, the Great Flood gave rise to a short-term ice age, and thereafter changed the world's climate dramatically. Such changes must have led to the extinction of dinosaurs.

The Bible records, in Genesis 1:21, that in the creation week God created "the great sea monsters" (NASB), too. This seems to be a reference to the huge sea monsters such as plesiosaurs which lived in the sea before the Great Flood. At the same time, a large variety of giant land creatures, such as dinosaurs, lived on land.

Further, in various places in the world, the fossils of huge ferns which were 30 to 40 meters (100 to 130 feet) high, as well as those of giant shellfish etc., have been discovered. The reason why such large plants and animals could survive was that, before the Great Flood, the water vapor canopy above the earth's atmosphere created a superb climatic environment.

Before the Great Flood, there was not a large variance in atmospheric temperature throughout the year, and the temperate climate meant that even giant living creatures had ample, constant supplies of food. Such a suitable living environment must have reduced stress levels in living creatures, and promoted the secretion of growth hormones.

Further, because of the water vapor canopy above the air before the Great Flood, the atmospheric pressure on the earth's surface must have been somewhat higher than the present-day levels. One creationist has calculated that the atmospheric pressure on the earth's surface before the Great Flood would have been about double that of modern-day levels.

At that time, there existed creatures such as giant dragonflies with wingspans of 80 to 100 centimeters (2.6 to 3.3 feet), as well as the reptilian Pteranodon which was also able to fly and had a wingspan of up to 6 meters (20 feet).

For such giant flying creatures, it would be extremely difficult to take off from flat ground under today's atmospheric pressure conditions. But, owing to the fact that the atmospheric pressure was about two times higher than today, it was much easier for them to fly in those days.

The evidence that the atmospheric pressure was high before the Great Flood is discovered in ancient amber, or fossil resin. Amber sometimes contains bubbles of air trapped so tightly that the air cannot escape. As the air bubble was formed concurrently with the resin, we can examine the bubble inside the ancient amber to find out about the atmosphere's condition in the distant past.

Examinations of ancient amber have also shown that the density of oxygen in the ancient air was higher than that of today's. The density of oxygen in today's atmosphere is about 21 percent, whereas it used to be about 30 percent in earlier ages. This higher density seems to have been due to the vigorous growth of plants on the earth before the Great Flood.

The abundant supply of oxygen must have helped animals to sustain healthy large body forms since, as recent research has evidenced, high oxygen pressure has a beneficial effect on the organs of living creatures.

Thus, the high atmospheric pressure and high oxygen pressure before the Great Flood undoubtedly contributed in no small way to the large size and long life of living creatures of that time.[18] However, following the Great Flood, the earth's climate underwent some drastic changes and the creatures which could not keep up with such changes became extinct.

Poikilothermal animals such as dinosaurs could not keep up with the changes after the Great Flood and became extinct.

Poikilothermal animals such as dinosaurs were among those living things which were unable to cope with the sudden environmental change.

The bodies of dinosaurs were so massive that, unlike other reptilian species, they were unable to protect themselves from the sudden drop in external temperatures by means of, for example, burying themselves in the ground and hibernating or warming themselves quickly once they cooled.

It appears that giant human species also lived before the Great Flood: many of the human footprints which were discovered in the vicinity of the Paluxy River in the U.S.A. measure about 40 centimeters (1.3 feet) long, and some have been reported to be even 50 centimeters (1.6 feet) (But other theory states that these footprints were of a dinosaur).[19] Additionally, the skeleton of a 2.13 meter (7 feet) tall human female has also been discovered in the basin of the Paluxy River, although it is not yet clear whether or not this relates to the giant footprints mentioned above.

But it does seem that giant people lived before the Great Flood. This may have some connection with the Biblical account appearing in Genesis 6:4 that: "The Nephilim [giants] were on the earth in those days [before the Great Flood]...."

The most notable climatic changes which occurred after the Great Flood include the polar regions becoming extremely cold, the gap between summer and winter temperatures becoming markedly wider, and the decrease in atmospheric pressure. Another change was that rainbows started to be seen sometimes after the rainfall.

By the way, ancient peoples believed that after rain fell from clouds in the sky, the water ran over the land and, once having found its way through rivers into the ocean, fell away into a giant waterfall which was believed to lie beyond the horizon.

Of course, modern-day man knows that this is not true. The water which goes to the ocean evaporates, producing moist air masses and clouds, which again release rain. In this manner, water rotates in the natural world through a cycle of:

cloud → rain → evaporation → cloud.

This is how the Bible speaks of the "water cycle":

"He (God) draws up the drops of water, which distill as rain to the streams; the clouds pour down their moisture and abundant showers fall on mankind. Who can understand how he spreads out the clouds, how he thunders from his pavilion?" (Job 36:27-29)

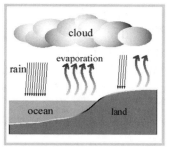

In this passage, the "water cycle" of evaporation ("...draws up the drops of water..."), condensation ("which distill..."), and rainfall ("as rain...") is splendidly described. Even from

Water rotates in the natural world through a cycle of "cloud → rain → evaporation → cloud."

the point of view of modern-day science, this description in the Bible is accurate, notwithstanding that it was written about 3000 years ago.

12. Fossils Formed by the Great Flood

LET US look at the relationship between the Great Flood and fossils.

For a long time, evolutionists have pointed to fossils found within the earth's strata as their strongest evidence in support of evolution theory.

Investigations of the earth's strata reveal that, in general, the fossils of simple living creatures are found in the deeper levels of the earth, and the higher the level is, the more fossils of complex living things can be discovered. To some extent, the principle of "simple, lower life-forms below; complicated, higher life-forms above" can be generally seen in the earth's strata.

Evolutionists claim this is a manifestation of each evolutionary stage, and they regard the arrangement of fossils as evidence of the gradual evolutionary development of living things. However, this arrangement of fossils does not indicate that living things evolved. The formation of fossils in the earth's strata is related not to evolution, but to Noah's Flood.

First, it is necessary to focus on the fact that fossils are most definitely not formed in a situation where the earth's strata accumulate very slowly over many years. Fossils can form only in the circumstance of some extreme, sudden disaster, such as the Great Flood. As a scientist has commented:

> "To become fossilized…It must be buried quickly to prevent decay and must be undisturbed throughout the long process."[20]

Assuming that soil accumulated very slowly over time, dead creatures would have rotted and decomposed before becoming fossilized, and would leave no skeletal frame. That is to say they would be "weathered" away. For example, when a fish dies, under no circumstances does it sink quietly to the ocean floor and become fossilized.

Neither does a dead land creature gradually become buried in the earth and become a fossil. Such creatures rot

Fossils are most definitely not formed in a situation where the earth's strata accumulate very slowly over many years.

and decompose before there is any chance of fossilization. Accordingly, the fact that fossils have been formed shows that the living creatures were subjected to some kind of extreme, sudden disaster which caused them to be buried quickly deep in the earth's strata to intercept the natural course of air and bacteria.

Noah's Great Flood provides the most reasonable explanation for this extreme, sudden disaster: the Flood caused each plant and animal to be suddenly buried, and preserved deep in the earth's strata under conditions of stable high pressure. Further, as the following discussion reveals, various scientific facts show that the earth's geological strata and the fossils found in them should be regarded as having resulted from a huge flood.

13. Earth's Strata Formation Due to Sudden Sediment Accumulation

Dr. Henry M. Morris, a hydraulics expert in the U.S.A., and the director of the Institute for Creation Research

(ICR), has concluded from his research that the earth's geological strata have not been formed over a long period, but formed within a short period as the result of the sudden accumulation of sediment:

> "Each distinctive stratum was laid down quickly, since it obviously represents a uniform set of water flow conditions, and such uniformity never persists very long. Each set of strata in a given formation must also have been deposited in rapid succession, or there would be evidence of unconformities—that is, periods of uplift and erosion—at the various interfaces."[21]

In other words, the earth's strata should be regarded as having formed very rapidly during one era. Further, it is indisputable that such formation was caused by the sudden accumulation of sediment resulting from a worldwide flood. In fact, as is commonly known, sedimentary rock (rock formed from the accumulation of sediment in water and water soluble matter) is found all over the world, and covers whole regions of all continents as well as seabeds. The average

Each stratum was laid down quickly. (Photo: Grand Canyon in the USA.)

depth of this sedimentary rock surrounding the whole earth is approximately 1.6 kilometers (1 mile).

Considering that the rate at which silt accumulates through compression under flood conditions is on average about 2.5 centimeters (1 inch) every five minutes, this means that the whole of the earth's strata could have formed in only 220 days.[22] [The Great Flood in Noah's time continued for more than 300 days. (Genesis 8:13)]

To many people, "1.6 kilometers" (1 mile) may sound very high, but it is about the same height as a medium-range mountain to be found anywhere all over the world; and compared with the diameter of the earth (12,756 kilometers or 7972 miles), it is a minuscule measurement. If a flood on a worldwide scale occurred, such an amount of accumulation would be very natural. America's Grand Canyon is famous for its wide-ranging exposure of deep levels of the earth's strata. Each of the Grand Canyon's strata spreads out evenly over a very wide area.

Geophysicists confirm that such an even distribution ranging over such a very wide area would be almost impossible if the earth's strata took hundreds or thousands of millions of years to be formed. During such a long period of time, there must have been some upheaval or folding to cause an irregular form. Moreover, analysis reveals many shortcomings in the evolutionist's "Geological Time-Table," and exposes the falseness of the idea that the earth's strata were formed over a long period.

When the Great Flood covered the earth, each layer of the earth's strata accumulated very rapidly, due to water currents that must have circled the earth several times. For this reason, the layers are not irregular but, rather, piled up evenly. Therefore, assuming that the earth's strata were formed in this way by the Great Flood, the arrangement of fossils within the earth's strata can be explained as follows:

14. Why "Simple, Lower Life-forms Below; Complex, Higher Life-forms Above"?

GENERALLY SPEAKING, in the lower levels of the earth, fossils of simple, lower life-forms are found; and the fossils of more complex, higher life-forms are uncovered closer to the surface. Why is this so?

Water has a "sifting action." Fine matter precipitates at the bottom, and larger matter settles further up. At the time of the Great Flood, the bodies of creatures were mixed together by the water currents, and thereafter settled and accumulated. At that time, finer, smaller living things settled below; and larger creatures precipitated above.

Microbes such as bacteria, inhabiting the ocean floor, settled in the lower layers and above them, the fossils of algae and shellfish species as well as other marine invertebrates were formed. As fishes and amphibians could swim, they accumulated higher up.

Animals having high degree of mobility moved to higher ground to escape from the Flood.

As for bird and mammal species, they lived at higher altitudes than marine life and, moreover, they were able to move to higher ground, as the water volume gradually increased during the rainy period preceding the Great Flood. Accordingly, their fossils are found at higher levels than those of marine creatures.

Human beings had the highest degree of mobility, combined with the knowledge of how to escape from water, which is why their fossils are generally found at the highest levels.

In fact, today we can see the impact of the Great Flood in large-scale excavations of fossils which have been made in various places throughout the world. In one place, several million fossils are piled up, and occasionally their form reveals that they were caught up in a final death struggle.

Sometimes these fossils are fish, sometimes mammals, and sometimes a mixture of both. They include the enormous quantities of hippopotamus bones found in Sicily, the large excavation of mammals in the Rocky Mountains, the excavations of dinosaurs in the Black Hills and Rocky Mountain ranges and the Gobi Desert, and the astonishing excavations of fish species in Scotland.

Why are the remains of these creatures found concentrated in such high places as the tops of mountains? Thomas F. Heinze, the author of *Creation vs. Evolution* has commented:

> "The water level gradually rises. Animals go in search of higher ground. Finally, they flock to the peaks of mountains. They are swept away and separated together with a mass of sediment."*[23]

In this way, animals with superior migratory abilities moved to high places in order to escape the rising water levels, and this is why their fossils are found in high places.

Accordingly, the fact that simple life-forms are usually found in the lower strata, and complex, higher life-forms are found in higher strata levels is not evidence of an evolutionary process, but is due to "the sifting action of water" and "the migration to high places of animals with migratory capabilities."

15. Why Do Fossils Appear Suddenly?

THE IDEA that geological strata and fossils were formed by the Great Flood adequately explains a large number of facts, which could not have been explained by evolutionist theory.

One example of this relates to the division by evolutionists of ages of time into "geological periods." Evolutionists apply various names, such as one period called "Cambrian Period," which is preceded by the so-called "Pre-Cambrian Period."

Evolutionists are puzzled by the fact that, in the stratum of the "Cambrian Period," various types of fossils can be found, while in the "Pre-Cambrian" stratum immediately below (the lowest stratum of all), multicellular fossils suddenly disappear. The textbook, *Stanfield's Science of Evolution*, states the following:

> "Representatives of almost all major groups of animals which are known today suddenly appear in the Cambrian period. It is as if a giant curtain was lifted to reveal a world thriving with life rich in change and abundantly fertile…This remains a problem today."*[24]

Thus, the fact that various kinds of fossils suddenly appear in the "Cambrian Period" stratum, whereas there are no identifiable fossils in the "Pre-Cambrian Period" is difficult to understand from the evolutionist's point of view, and this "remains a problem today" to the theory of evolution.

However, this issue can be easily understood from a creationist perspective. Assuming that sediments resulting from the Great Flood accumulated just above the pre-flood stratum (which evolutionists call the "Pre-Cambrian" stratum), and formed the earth's strata, it is natural that various fossils are suddenly to be found above that level.

This idea also explains why, all over the world, the interface between the "Cambrian" and "Pre-Cambrian" stratum is "unconformable" (not continuous). As the authors of *The History of the Earth*, professors Shoji Ijiri and Masao Minato in Japan, have written:

> "Examinations of Cambrian Period stratum in various parts of the world reveals that this stratum lies mostly level, on top of Pre-Cambrian stratum which underwent violent degeneration or folding…The relationship between the Cambrian period stratum and the stratum preceding it is unconformable, no matter where in the world one investigates, and no place has ever been found to be conformable. One might well wonder as to the significance of this fact."[25]

As this statement describes, very evident doubts arise from the fact of this "unconformity." Every upper stratum lies level, and the lowest stratum undulates violently—rises and falls—everywhere in the world. This means that the formation of the lowest stratum and the strata above it did not occur continuously, but was interrupted by a gap in time.

Evolutionists cannot sufficiently explain the significance of this worldwide "unconformity," but it can be understood as a very natural phenomenon, in the event that the higher strata were formed as a result of the Great Flood.

16. Various Facts Explained by the Great Flood

THE GREAT FLOOD can explain many other facts in addition to the above, which evolutionist theory cannot explain.

One example is the fossils of trees. Among the tree fossils discovered, there exist some highly prized examples which extend through several strata. Some tree fossils are standing

Tree fossils with trunks are extending through several strata were found in France, Australia, and many other places.

perfectly straight even now, some are slanting, and others are upside down, but their trunks are extending through several strata! It gives the unmistakable appearance of the sudden layering of accumulated strata around trees which were caught in an overflow of water.

This phenomenon cannot possibly be explained by the evolutionist idea, because evolutionists think that the strata were formed very slowly over an extremely long period of time. For creationists, it is one strong piece of evidence that the strata were formed very rapidly as the result of the Great Flood.

Again, according to evolutionists, one can expect to discover the fossils of only simple, inferior life-forms in the lower, supposedly older strata—but never the fossils of high level life-forms. However, the fossils of relatively high-level life-forms are in fact sometimes found in the lower strata. In places all over the world, the evolutionists' geological order in their "Age-Table" is sometimes quite the reverse.

This is so, notwithstanding that the interface is perfectly conformable between the geological strata which have shifted their order. Those strata reveal no trace of dislocation, slipping, or movement above or under other strata. Every stratum accumulated consecutively.

This fact has perplexed evolutionists, but it is totally consistent with the idea that the earth's strata were formed by the Great Flood; i.e., there must have been some creatures that failed to migrate to higher ground at the time of the Great

Flood and were soon overcome by the rising water. Their bodies were caught up in the lower strata.

Assuming the formation of strata as a result of the Great Flood, it is perfectly reasonable to expect the fossils of relatively higher life-forms to be found sometimes in the lower strata.

The attempt by evolution theory to explain the origins of oil and coal has also met with many difficulties but, once again, if there was a Great Flood as recorded in the Bible, the explanation for such matters becomes extremely simple.

According to the results of analyses by modern-day scientists, it is thought that oil is the transformed remains of large quantities of ancient marine animals, especially plankton and microbes. There is nothing among the events which occur in today's natural world to explain how the corpses of a large quantity of them came to be accumulated like this within the earth's geological strata.

It is feasible to argue that most of the oil, which is extracted in places all over the world today, is actually the transformed corpses of creatures that were buried as a result of the Great Flood.

Creationists reason that coal is produced from trees and other vegetation, which were uprooted by the fury of the Great Flood, swept away by the force, accumulated, transformed by the heat of the earth into coal, and now dug out.

Thus, the Great Flood explains a variety of facts relating to the earth's strata and fossils, much more adequately than evolutionist theory.

17. Continents Were Once One Landmass

NEXT, let us look more closely at the drastic changes which occurred to the topographical shape of the earth following the Great Flood.

The theory that "the continents which are scattered over the earth today were once joined as a whole" is prevalent among today's scientists.

At the beginning of the twentieth century, a German scientist A. Wegener was gazing at the world globe, and noticed that the western coastlines of the continents of Europe and Africa were very similar to the shape of the eastern coastlines of the North and South American continents.

In other words, he noticed that the outlines of continents lying on both sides of the Atlantic Ocean, if aligned together, fit each other almost perfectly. He also knew that the same kinds of fossils had been found in Africa and South America.

Wegener thus reasoned that both these continents might have originally been joined together. Having regard to various other considerations, he then pronounced his theory that all continents were originally attached as one whole, and then separated, by "drifting" apart to their present positions (the "Continental Drift Theory").

The coastlines of both sides of the Atlantic Ocean are very similar.

At one stage, this theory was opposed by several opposing theories but, thereafter, the persuasive value of Wegener's theory was reappraised, and nowadays his theory is referred to extensively. The idea that continents were once joined together accords with the Biblical account in Genesis 1:9:

> "And God said, Let the water under the sky be gathered to one place, and let dry ground appear: And it was so."

It can thus be understood that, at the time of creation, water was concentrated in one place forming one large ocean, and one "ground" appeared. There was one large landmass. If one accepts that the continents were once joined together as one whole, the next question is how they came to be separated.

According to the Bible, continents before the Great Flood were not only joined together but also the undulation (ups and downs) of the land was much more gentle in comparison with the present. However, after the occurrence of the Great Flood, various changes took place to the cooled earth's crust, when "the mountains rose; the valleys sank down" (Psalm 104:8 NASB). (Many of the translations go like this. Still some translations read, "[the waters] flowed over the mountains, they went down into the valleys." This does not accurately reflect the original Hebrew.)

Owing to such rising of mountains, and sinking down of valleys, the shape of the continents changed substantially. There must have been places in which land, previously above sea level before the Great Flood, became submerged by it and, similarly, land under water became uncovered. In this way, the shape of the former whole landmass was dramatically altered, and itself became divided.

Therefore, according to the Bible, the separation of continents occurred, not simply due to "slow drifting," but mainly due to the elevation of mountains and the depression of valleys, which was caused by the forces of the Great Flood. There is ample evidence available in support of this idea. For example, the flood-accumulated strata which can be observed in England, and the northeast regions of America are surprisingly similar, and this strongly suggests that these two landmasses were once joined together.

However, in the ocean basin (a large depression at the bottom of the ocean) of the Atlantic Ocean which ties these two landmasses, there are no such flood-accumulated strata. This reveals that these continental masses must have separated after the Great Flood. As Professor Stuart E. Nevins has commented:

"The cause for the ancient breaking up of continents can be explained easily by the enormous
catastrophic forces of Noah's Flood."[26]

In this manner, the continental landmass was originally
unified but, due to the catastrophic forces to the land caused
by the Great Flood, it separated into several sections.

It is also thought that the continents now continue to
grow further apart from each other by about several centimeters a year. Modern scientists think that the outer lithospheric
shell of the earth consists of a mosaic of rigid "plates," and
continents move slowly lying on these plates, due to the influence of the movements below in the earth's mantle.

The Japanese archipelago is also said to be moving, by a
very small degree, further away from the Eurasian continent.
This is how the continents and islands have come to be settled
in their present-day shape and location.

18. Jerusalem: Appointed Center of All Nations

IT APPEARS that God's special consideration was accorded
to the process of separation, at the time when the continents
became divided.

Some very interesting facts have been uncovered by the
investigation undertaken by certain scientists in respect of the
"center point of all landmasses" on the surface of the earth, or
the "center of all nations," which involves deducing the center
of all landmasses on the earth's spherical surface, without
changing their current shapes and positions.

This research has been chiefly undertaken by Dr.
Andrew J. Woods, an American physicist. The method
employed in such research involves "dividing of all land mass
into very small parts, and searching for the spot at which the
sum total of distance to all other divided portions becomes
smallest."

For all practical purposes, this spot is regarded mathematically as the geographical center of all landmass on the earth. Computers were used to make this calculation, since it involves not only continental landmasses but also islands, and is very complicated.

What was the result of that study? It was made apparent that the region from Palestine to Mesopotamia is the center of all landmasses, namely, the region containing the Tower of Babel, Bethlehem, Nazareth, Jerusalem, or, in other words, the area which was the stage for all major events of the Bible.[27]

In fact, this area is the "point of contact" for the three major continents of Europe, Asia, and Africa; and also the "point of intersection" of regions inhabited by Caucasoid, Mongoloid, and Negroid races respectively.

The fact that Israel is located at the center of the world has, astonishingly, been recorded in the Bible already about 2600 years ago. In chapter 5, verse 5 of the Book of Ezekiel, it states:

> "This is what the Sovereign Lord says: This is Jerusalem, which I have set in the center of the nations, with countries all around her."

And again, Ezekiel 38:12 refers to the People of Israel as "living at the center of the land." Thus the Bible, during an age in which man's knowledge of geography was in an extremely infantile stage, describes the state of Israel as the center of the nations and, moreover, reveals that this was in fact planned by God.

The division and reformation of continents occurred to let Jerusalem become the center of all landmasses.

Furthermore, according to the Bible passages just quoted, the earth's center is not only Israel but Israel's Holy City Jerusalem, where Christ was crucified for our redemption.

Thus, God purposefully placed Jerusalem at the center of all nations for all people. When God divided the once united continents, he arranged that the land point to be known in the future as Jerusalem would become the center of the earth. That is, the earth's landmass was separated into pre-determined places. The Bible records:

> "[After the Great Flood] the mountains rose; the valleys sank down to the place which Thou didst establish for them." (Psalm 104:8 NASB)

Further,

> "Thou didst set a boundary that they (waters) may not pass over." (Psalm 104:9)

Thus, the elevation and depression and breaking up of the land was planned in order to create a preordained coast-line. In other words, it was carried out to obtain a preordained topography and predetermined results. This is how the present day topography came about, and how Jerusalem came to be positioned at the center of the earth. There can be no doubt that in God's heart alone was the plan that the Gospel should originate in Jerusalem and spread all over the world.

19. Revival of Catastrophism

AS WE HAVE learned so far, the condition of the earth before the Great Flood was quite different from the present day in various aspects including atmospheric conditions, topography, and ecology of living things.

However, after the Great Flood, atmospheric conditions and climate underwent drastic change, the surface of the earth was reshaped, and ecological aspects also changed. This idea of drastic change in the earth's history is called "Catastrophism."

Catastrophism is supported by extensive scientific evidence, and offers the most forceful explanation with respect to the past condition of the earth. Moreover, this idea compels some major revisions of past evolutionist theory relating to the age of the earth and of mankind.

In fact, the period of time dating from mankind's appearance on the earth to the present day is not as long as traditional evolutionist notions imply, and we will explore this matter later in this book. Catastrophism is an important idea which is a pillar of creationist theory.

In the past, catastrophism was widely accepted in the Middle Ages in Europe, etc., as one of the tenets of the Christian faith, although at that time this theory was not backed by any scientific knowledge, and was thus extremely vague.

In the nineteenth century, Cuvier, a French scientist, advanced a unique theory of catastrophism. Based on his interpretation of fossils within the earth's strata, he postulated that there have until now occurred "repeated" catastrophes, which have resulted each time in the annihilation of the greater part of living species, and led to the creation of new living things.

He then advocated that "Noah's Great Flood" was the last of such catastrophes. However, Cuvier's theory does not sit well with the various scientific evidences available today, nor does it accord with the Bible.

Cuvier's theory was later abandoned and, in place of it, "Uniformitarianism" became prevalent. Uniformitarianism is the theory that does not acknowledge any sudden or catastrophic change in the past, but emphasizes the slow, uniform processes of the present as a sufficient explanation for all aspects of history and the structures of the earth.

Uniformitarianism is often expressed in the phrase, "The present is the key to the past." It is based on the idea that everything about history of the earth can be adequately explained by reference to gradual processes of change such as those we see in the present day world.

Using this hypothesis as their foundation, evolutionists proposed that the earth itself and life thereon evolved very slowly over a long period of time. Thus, evolutionist theory effectively grew out of uniformitarianism.

It appears that, behind the spread of uniformitarianism was the thought that it would act as an extremely convenient base for advancing evolutionist theory, as well as other motivations such as a biased view of Biblical accounts of creation as being merely mythical. In addition, the fact that Cuvier's catastrophism was incomplete and lacked persuasive power also promoted the spread of the uniformitarianism.

From the nineteenth century to the present day, uniformitarianism has gained a stronghold in the popular consciousness, but this was, most surprisingly, predicted in advance by the Bible, which states:

> "First of all, you must understand that in the last days scoffers will come…They will say: Where is this 'coming' he promised? Ever since our fathers died, everything goes on as it has since the beginning of creation." (II Peter 3:3-4)

The idea that "Everything goes on as it has since the beginning of creation" is surely at the heart of uniformitarianism. It has been anticipated in the Bible that this theory would come to achieve a certain degree of force. However, the Bible continues:

> "But they deliberately forget that long ago…By these waters also the world of that time was deluged and destroyed." (II Peter 3:5-6)

In other words, the Bible supports catastrophism, rather than uniformitarianism, as the proper theory for understanding the past history of the earth.

The revised catastrophism which I mention in this book was first advanced by some American scientists who were creationists. As defects in uniformitarianism have become more apparent these days, this new catastrophism has been accepted by many people, and continues to be the object of ongoing research. Just as evolutionist theory is built on uniformitarianism, so is creationist theory based on catastrophism.

It is apparent that at some time in earth history, the earth has undergone change so drastic as to largely transform the conditions of the earth at that time, including atmospheric conditions, climate, topography, and the ecology of living things.

Without acknowledging such a drastic change, it is impossible to discuss the history of this planet and of living things. There can be no doubt that such change was brought about by the Great Flood in Noah's time, as recorded in the Bible.

In this connection, let us look at some of the questions which are commonly asked in relation to Noah's ark.

20. What Kind of Vessel Was Noah's Ark?

ACCORDING TO the Bible, Noah's ark was about 300 cubits (140 meters or 450 feet) long (based on the conversion rate of 1 cubit = 46 centimeters), 50 cubits (23 meters or 75 feet) wide, and 30 cubits (14 meters or 45 feet) high (Genesis 6:15), so it was a very enormous craft, comparable to a large modern cruise liner.

As the ark required no navigational capacity, being required merely to stay afloat, it was probably box-like in shape, and not streamlined like today's modern vessels. With

© Creation Magazine Illustration: Steve Cardno

Noah's ark had length, width, and height dimensions in the proportions of 30:5:3, which afforded the highest degree of stability and safety.

length, width, and height in proportions of 30:5:3, its shape was relatively oblong and flat. If a sea craft is too short, its stability decreases, but if it is too long, there is a danger that the vessel may break in the middle when it encounters high waves. The same thing can be said about the height and width.

Shipbuilding experts have described a shape in the ratio of 30:5:3 as a design of superior safety, and extremely high degree of stability.

Mr. Shinto, who was the Chairman of NTT (telegraph & telephone company in Japan), was formerly the president of a shipbuilding company, and at that time he commanded a research team to investigate the ideal shape for large-sized sea craft. The result of their study was that, for large sea craft in the tanker class, the shape which affords the highest degree of stability and safety is that having length, width, and height dimensions in the proportions of 30:5:3.

These are called "golden proportions," by which sea craft is never overturned or broken even on the raging ocean. Following this finding, this shape has largely become the standard in the shipbuilding world for tanker class large-sized sea craft. This is the same shape as Noah's ark, which Noah built at God's direction.

Noah's ark was designed with a window in the upper deck, and a doorway at the side. The interior consisted of three levels, partitioned into several rooms. The timber used in the construction of the partition-walls must have contributed to the strength of the vessel. "Gopher wood" was used in such construction, and was precoated with pitch in order to make it waterproof.

Thus, the ark was extremely well designed in preparation for the Great Flood. Moreover, one can only marvel at the construction of such an enormous sea craft in the middle of land, during a time when there was no recorded shipbuilding technology. Such an achievement became possible owing to the instruction from God (Genesis 6:15).

21. Could All Species Be Contained in the Ark?

ACCORDING TO the Bible, seven pairs (a male and its mate) of every kind of "clean animal"(able to be eaten), one pair of every kind of "unclean animal" (not able to be eaten) living on land, and seven pairs of each kind of bird entered the ark (Genesis 7:2-9). Thus, each type of land animal and bird was contained in the ark.

It is often a subject of debate as to how each one of the large variety of types of animals could have possibly been contained in the ark. Taking dogs as one example, there is a wide range of breeds, including German shepherd, St. Bernard, spaniel, collie, and retriever, just to name a few. It is the same with respect to cats, horses, cows, monkeys, elephants, and so on. Thus, it is argued that Noah could never have fitted such a wide range of animals into the ark, even if he tried.

However, it was not necessary for Noah to go that far; he merely had to include one representative of each variety of animal, since each living thing has its own "gene pool," which makes it possible for "variation" to occur as the genes are passed from generation to generation.

It is known that dogs such as German shepherds, St. Bernards, spaniels, etc., which were mentioned earlier, although they appear externally very different, in fact, belong to the same one "species," and are derived as a result of "variation" from their common ancestor before them.

The three basic types of humankind (Caucasoid, Mongoloid, and Negroid) have also come from one original ancestral couple through such a process of variation. The Bible records that the people who boarded Noah's ark comprised only Noah, his wife, his three sons, and their wives.

The entire human species existing today, including the basic three types of humankind mentioned earlier, is derived from them. The genes within their "gene pool" were the only necessary ingredients for producing a wide variety of humankind.

The term "variation" is used to apply to the capacity of living things such as dogs, cats, and human beings to vary from one original type to a variety of different types within the species. However, such changes can never occur so as to exceed the boundaries of the species.

The variation can occur only to the extent that the living thing remains within its species. Thus, it was sufficient for Noah to include in the ark only representatives of each species. Furthermore, he did not need to include any aquatic animals; he took only land animals in.

As for dinosaurs, he did not need to choose an enormous adult sample of the species. He could have selected newborns or teenagers. Dinosaurs are born from eggs, and their babies are very small.

Species of land animals which are larger than sheep are estimated to number no more than three hundred, even considering extinct ones; the ark's total floor space of about 9000 square meters would have been enough to accommodate all of them.

Thus, it can be reasoned that the wide variety of animals which can be seen in the world today have derived, through the process of "variation," from the representative animals which Noah put into the ark.

22. Has Noah's Ark Been Discovered?

ACCORDING TO the Bible, Noah's ark became grounded on a peak in the mountains of Armenia, called Ararat.

At the base of Mt. Ararat is the city of Naxuana or Nakhichevan, which claims the tomb of Noah. The name means "Here Noah settled."

Some publications report that just before the outbreak of the Russian revolution in 1917, Russian aviators announced having seen the hulk of a gigantic ship high up in the inaccessible glacier fastnesses of Mt. Ararat.

The Russian czar received news of this sighting and organized a team of explorers, who discovered the vessel, measured its dimensions, sketched, and photographed it. However, at that time the Russian government was overthrown by atheist revolutionaries, and the report of the explorers was never published.[28]

In 1955, a French mountain climber, Fernand Navarra, discovered a piece of old, crafted wood, beneath the perpetual ice at a point near the top of the mountains of Ararat about 4300 meters (14100 feet) above sea level. He said, "I discovered Noah's Ark."

He published a book about it, which aroused widespread discussion. The age of the wood he found was investigated by

Navarra discovered a piece of old, crafted wood, beneath the perpetual ice at a point near the top of the mountains of Ararat.

both the Madrid Institute for Forestry Studies and the Bordeaux University Natural Science Department, and was estimated to be about 3000 to 5000 years old (the Great Flood was about 4500 years ago).[29]

After that, there were several reports of photographs of ship-like structures having been taken on Mt. Ararat. However, owing to an earthquake which occurred on Mt. Ararat, some have suggested that Noah's Ark is now buried somewhere deep in the mountain. In any case, there is no decisive evidence available to persuade a large number of people with respect to this question.

Climbing or surveying of Mt. Ararat is hindered by political restraints, and practical impairments such as the fact that the area around the summit is usually closed off by ice. Thus, we can only hope for a thoroughgoing investigation of the mountain to be undertaken in the near future.

23. Could Today's World Population Have Possibly Derived from Eight People?

IN 1987, the world population exceeded five billion. One might well ask whether it is at all possible for this population to have been derived, in the period from the Great Flood to the present day, from those eight survivors of the Great Flood who were aboard Noah's ark (Noah, his wife, his three sons, and their wives).

Assuming that the period of time from the Great Flood to the present day is about 4500 years, and that during that time the population increased from eight people to five billion, the rate at which the population grew is about equal to doubling every 150 years.

In the twentieth century, in the middle of 1920's, the world population was about two billion. Then, only about 50 years later, in 1974, the population doubled to four billion. Again, the world population was about 3 billion in 1960. Only about 40 years later, in 2000, the population doubled to six billion.

Thus, the world population has risen very sharply in the twentieth century. But even assuming that the population growth of previous ages was slower than this, the period from the Great Flood to the present day was certainly sufficient time for the world population to grow from eight people to its current level.

24. The Great Flood and Age of Trees

I MENTIONED that the Great Flood occurred about 4500 years ago. Is there any evidence of this in the world, besides the verses in the Bible? There is. Trees provide us with such evidence. Trees have the longest life among all living things on the earth. For instance, it is common for the giant sequoia trees in America to reach an age of several thousand years.

In the towering forests of these trees, any tree you care to choose will have a diameter of about 10 meters (33 feet), and pinecones measuring 30 centimeters or so (1 foot) can be found here and there on the forest floor. The forests are so huge that people standing in the midst of these trees are made to feel like dwarfs.

What is the natural life span of trees? It is said that the life span of trees is almost limitless. Biologists say that trees will live for tens of thousands of years when given the right conditions. However, the oldest tree on the earth today is about 4500 years old.

It is the tree called *Pinus aristata*, commonly known as the bristlecone pine, which still grows in the mountain districts of California, U.S.A. You will not find an older tree on the earth, even if you search the world over. This tree is the oldest living thing with the longest life span on the earth.

It is worthy to note that there are no living things over 4500 years old. In fact, 4500 years ago was about the time of

Noah's Great Flood, which covered the whole earth and uprooted all trees. This oldest tree must have sprouted buds just after the Great Flood.

25. About the Flood Layer in Mesopotamia

WITH RESPECT to Noah's Great Flood, I have explained that there are two theories: the "Local Flood Theory" (that the flood was confined to the basin of the Tigris and Euphrates rivers), and the "Worldwide Flood Theory" (that the flood covered the whole earth). Let us look at this subject a little further.

The grounds for the local flood theory are based on the discovery of a "flood layer" over a wide area in the basin of the Tigris and Euphrates rivers. Archaeologists Dr. C. L. Wooley and Dr. Stephen Langdon investigated strata at the basin of the Tigris and Euphrates, such as Ur, Kish, Fara, and Nineveh, and discovered a great, solid, water-laid stratum several meters thick without admixture of human relic. Moreover, beneath that stratum lie the remains of another city.

It is estimated that the stratum has been formed by a widespread flood over an area of 480 kilometers x 160 kilometers (300 miles by 100 miles), and these archaeologists reasoned that the flood in question was the Great Flood in Noah's time. How might this flood layer be understood from the point of view of the worldwide flood theory? This flood layer can only be the result of overflowing of the Tigris and Euphrates rivers, which occurred after Noah's Great Flood.

The Great Flood began when the water vapor canopy above the atmosphere began to fall as heavy rain, leading to the formation of geological strata over the whole earth. There can be no doubt that the flood layer of Mesopotamia is the stratum which was formed, as a result of the overflow of the Tigris and Euphrates rivers, on top of the strata which had previously resulted from Noah's Flood.

If the flood area had been limited, then it would have been impossible for it to "cover all the high places," and to continue flooding for "150 days" (Genesis 7:24). Also, as I mentioned earlier, if the flood was local, Noah had no need to construct the ark; he could have just sought refuge in an area beyond the reaches of the floodwaters.

Moreover, we know that if we take into account matters such as the fact that the legends of the Great Flood can be seen almost all over the world, and that the idea of a worldwide flood soundly explains the formation of the earth's strata and of fossils, the suggestion that Noah's Flood was worldwide is revealed to be patently reasonable.

26. Fossils Formed Within a Short Period

IN ORDER FOR living things to become fossilized, a long period of time such as several hundred million years, or even tens of thousands of years is not necessary. The bodies of living things will not fossilize unless they are suddenly buried and placed in high-pressure conditions. In the case of such a sudden burial, under high-pressure conditions, their remains will become fossilized in a relatively short period.

Fossilization is really the process whereby the remains of living creatures become "stone," but this is merely one of the chemical changes. When intensely high pressure is applied, the material can transform into something with completely different properties.

A good example of this is the artificial diamond, which is formed by compacting charcoal by applying intense pressure. The charcoal which is used for burning as well as real diamonds are made from the same carbon, but have completely different properties.

To make artificial diamonds from charcoal does not require an enormously long time such as tens of thousands of years, but can in fact be produced in a relatively short time period. It is the same with naturally occurring diamonds. Their formation does not require a long time period such as hundreds of millions of years. As a matter of fact, artificial diamonds have recently been successfully produced from peanut butter.

The principle of fossils is exactly the same as this. Through the medium of pressure, the bodies of living things and the properties of matter undergo change, and become stone. If pressure is added, then a period of millions of years is not necessary in order to effect fossilization. Fossils could be formed within several months.

Creationists believe that the fossils which are excavated in regions all over the world today were formed mostly as a result of the Great Flood in the days of Noah. The Great Flood suddenly buried all of the creatures existing at that time, and locked them away under a deep cover of silt and water.

The remains of those creatures were fossilized during a relatively short time period thereafter, due to the extraordinary pressure of such water and silt. It has not taken a long period of time, in the order of millions of years, for these to be fossilized.

✦

Chapter Four

The Age of Man and Planet Earth

1. Mankind Is Millions of Years Old?

FINALLY, let us consider the age of the earth and of human beings. How many years have passed since the birth of the earth and of humankind? This question is the source of great controversy among evolutionists and creationists.

How old do evolutionists regard the earth and human beings? Some evolutionist texts state:

"the earth was formed approximately 4.5 billion years ago."[1]

"Our human ancestors were finally born over two million and some hundreds of thousands of years ago."[2]

However, there is room for doubt as to the reliability of these huge estimations. Let us first look at the question of the age of man, and then at the age of the earth.

The so-called "carbon-14" ("C-14" or "carbon dating") method is commonly used at present for dating the past. This method was invented by Willard F. Libby, for which he received a Nobel prize in 1960.

The C-14 method is regarded highly also by creationists, and its reliability has been confirmed dating back some 4000 years ago, through comparison and amendment with archaeological writing and materials, the age of which is already known. Libby states:

> "Both dates (the date of archaeological materials and the date ascertained by the C-14 method) are consistent up to 4000 years ago."*[3]

As there are no archaeological materials dating back beyond 4000 years, it is impossible to check the accuracy of this method beyond such time. However, the C-14 method is generally considered to be quite reliable.

By using this method, Libby studied human fossils, and estimated their age. What was the result of such study? Did he estimate the age of man to be in the order of "millions of years"? No! The result was quite different from such huge estimations. According to Libby's treatise which appeared in the *American Journal of Physics*, the age of man, as established through the examination of various human remains, is at most about 20,000 to 40,000 years.[4]

Dr. E. Hallonquist has also commented as follows, concerning a variety of specimens which have been examined through the C-14 method.

> "A skull which has been regarded as one of the oldest fossils of Homo sapiens (estimated by

evolutionists to be about 200,000 to 300,000 years old) is estimated by the C-14 method to be no more than 8,500 years old.

"While the skull of the Australopithecus is officially reported to be 1 million to 2 million years old, the bone of an animal found at the same location where Australopithecus was found, in the Omo valley of Ethiopia, is estimated as only 15,500 years old according to the C-14 method...

"The bone of a mammalian animal at Olduvai Gorge in Tanzania, Africa, where Zinjanthropus has been discovered, is officially reported to date back about 2 million years, but in fact, according to the C-14 method, it can be no more than 11,000 years old."[5]

The fossils which evolutionists have estimated to date back an extraordinarily long period of time are, in fact, only 20,000 years or less, according to the C-14 method.

He continues:

"If you go to a university library, select a copy of the magazine *Radiocarbon*, and read it, you can substantiate the above mentioned facts. You may be surprised to see the dates recorded in that magazine, and the results of the various studies.

"Using the C-14 method, hundreds of scientists dated fossils of so-called prehistoric animals, such as those of Neanderthal man, CroMagnon man, Broken Hill man, mammoths, mastodons, tigers with well-developed canine teeth like a saber, other extinct animals, as well as fossilized trees, wood, coal, oil, natural gas, and found them to be only several thousands of years old."*6

What does this mean? The fossils which evolutionists have estimated to date back an extraordinarily long period of time are, in fact, only 20,000 years or less, according to the C-14 method.

This is not an error due to numerical misprint. According to the C-14 method, the age of humankind is no more than 20,000 years. On what basis, did evolutionists base their figure of "millions of years"?

2. Evolutionists Selected a Result to Match Evolution Theory

A NEWSPAPER reported as follows, regarding a fragment of fossilized elbow bone which was discovered in 1967:

"A bone discovered in Kenya reveals human age to be 2.5 million years."

How did evolutionists arrive at this figure of "2.5 million years"? It was calculated according to the "potassium-argon" dating method. This method is the same as the carbon dating method insofar as it utilizes radioactive isotopes but, practically speaking, the two methods are totally different.

Whereas the carbon dating method directly examines the actual fossil, the potassium-argon method, which is not by its nature able to do this, examines instead the volcanic rock which is discovered in the closest proximity to the fossil.

The date determined by potassium-argon method is thus the date when the volcanic rock cooled down and hardened, and this date is then regarded as the date of the actual fossil. However, there are crucial doubts as to the reliability of the potassium-argon method.

The half-life period of radioactive potassium, which is the basis for the potassium-argon dating method, is 1,300,000,000 (1.3 billion) years. Over such an incredible period of time, half of potassium turns into argon. By measuring this ratio of potassium to argon, the potassium-argon method attempts to determine the date.

Thus, whether the subject fossil is thousands of years or even millions of years old, the dating by potassium-argon method will, since its half-life is very different in figures, be as if "timing a second by a clock that has only an hour hand": one can never expect an accurate outcome.

Additionally, this method is based on a number of flimsy assumptions while there are various reports from around the world which indicate that its dating results are extremely inaccurate and unreliable. Professor Minoru Kojima of Tokyo University has stated in this regard:

> "The Potassium-argon method is known as having a tendency to produce very ancient dates, which are, of course, totally unrelated to the true dates…(and) it also has a basic flaw in that it is very difficult to check whether the dates by this method are in fact the actual dates of the rock in question."[7]

For example, the result of measurement by potassium-argon method of certain lava, which is known to have formed from 1800 to 1801 at a volcano in Hawaii, appeared in a science magazine published in 1968.

Considering that the half-life of radioactive potassium is 1.3 billion years, and that they dated the lava from 170 years ago, the only possible result must be next to zero. However, the magazine reported that the lava was dated as 160 million to 3 billion years old, and asked how this result should be regarded.[8]

In the journal, *Science* of Oct. 11, 1968, it was reported that volcanic rocks, which were known to be less than 200 years old, were dated as 12 million to 21 million years old.[9] Similar results have been reported from all over the world, including Norway, Germany, Japan, France, and Russia, indicating that the dates yielded by potassium-argon method are in fact much older than the actual dates.

Additionally, *Australopithecus*, which evolutionists call the "ape-man" or the oldest human fossil, was excavated by the famous Dr. Richard Leakey, and it was estimated, according to the potassium-argon method, to be 2.6 million years old. However, according to the age-dating specialist, Professor E. T. Hull, *Australopithecus* was first estimated by potassium-argon method as being 220 million years old.

This initial result was rejected just because it was regarded as unrealistically old, and an alternative rock specimen was chosen for testing. This specimen yielded a more acceptable result of 2.6 million years, and this figure was finally adopted.[10]

As these facts reveal, evolutionists have chosen only those results which conform to evolution theory, and have ignored conflicting results. Thus, we can only conclude that the dates adopted by evolutionists are ill grounded and unreliable.

3. The Age of Man is 6000 Years

EVOLUTIONISTS, once they realized that the results derived by the C-14 method did not concur with evolution theory, came up with the results by potassium-argon method and adopted them. This was not because the potassium-argon method was found to be reliable, but simply because such results better suit their evolution theory, which is premised on long periods of the earth's history.

Generally speaking, evolutionists tend to accept the method that yields the oldest dates, since they are possessed by the idea that humankind has required ages of time to evolve. As Dr. Henry M. Morris comments:

> "The evidence of evolution rests merely on the assumption of evolution."*

If one assumes that human beings did not evolve from inferior life-forms, but rather were created as human beings in the first place, then there is no necessity to regard such creation as having occurred many millions of years ago.

Such creationist positions can be well explained in terms of known scientific facts. The most reliable evidence at hand today indicates that a long period of time has not passed since the birth of mankind. In fact, there is reason to believe that the age of man estimated by the C-14 method to be about "20,000 years," as mentioned earlier, is even much greater than the true age. This is because the C-14 method is premised on a very particular assumption, that "the amount of C-14 in the atmosphere has been constant throughout all ages."

If this assumption is not prescribed, then it is impossible to make correct estimations. But if there was a drastic change in the earth's history, such as a massive flood, then this assumption does not hold. One would expect the amount of C-14 in the atmosphere to have changed when the Great Flood occurred.

Before the Great Flood, as mentioned earlier, there was an extensive water vapor canopy called "the water above the expanse" (Genesis 1:7), which covered the earth and the atmosphere. This water vapor canopy impeded the penetration of cosmic rays, and thus reduced the amount of C-14 which is generated in the atmosphere by cosmic rays.

In relation to this, hard evidence was discovered by the American geologist, Dr. Landes. He investigated the air shut up in ancient amber, which is fossil resin, and analyzed it to understand the condition of the ancient atmosphere. He found that the amount of C-14 in the ancient atmosphere was much less than the present day.

Assuming that the amount of C-14 was lower in the ages before the Great Flood, what kind of effect would this have on the estimation of dates? A scientific magazine comments:

> "If the amount of C-14 in the atmosphere was less than today, the estimation which we get as the period since the time when a particular creature lived must be too long."

In other words, if we estimate by the C-14 method the date of creatures which lived before the Great Flood, we arrive at a date which is much older than the actual one. Accordingly, the actual age of mankind must be far less than 20,000 years.

Based on a literal interpretation of the Bible, the creation of man took place only about 6000 years ago. One can find general support for this Biblical figure in the order of 6000 years, as the age of mankind, including the results yielded by the C-14 method.

4. Limits to the Age of the Earth

NEXT, let us look at the age of the earth, which evolutionists have put at 4.5 billion or 4.6 billion years.

Even between the nineteenth century and the beginning of the twentieth century, scientists had presented various evidence in support of the proposition that the age of the earth was no more than 100 million years old in the extreme, and certainly not so incredibly old as today's estimates by evolutionists.

One such piece of evidence, for example, was the estimation related to the "saltiness of the sea." Ocean salt is carried to the ocean bit by bit through rivers flowing from the continents. Thus, on the presumption that both now and in the past salt has been carried from the rivers to the ocean at the same speed, it is possible to estimate the time it took for ocean salt density to attain its current levels.

As explained earlier, creationists, who recognize that there was a drastic change due to the Great Flood, argue that most of the density of today's ocean salt can be attributed to the mixing of sediment in the ocean as a result of the Great Flood.

However, let us consider whether or not an estimate of "several billion years" is yielded, by not acknowledging the drastic change and assuming rather, as the evolutionists do, that ocean salt has increased at the same slow pace over time. In fact, even by this analysis, the result is about "100 million years." Moreover, this estimate is thought to be at the "high end of the scale," which indicates that the ocean is at most this old, but no older.[11]

This result is based on the assumption that the speed at which salt is carried has been the same throughout the ages. But actually it must have been faster in the past: the speed must have decreased to current-day levels, resulting in the decrease of salt density in the earth's soil. Therefore, it is very reasonable to think that the age of the ocean is far less than 100 million years.

As both evolutionists and creationists think that the ocean was born just after the primitive earth was made, the age of the earth, too, must be less than "100 million years."

Assuming that the earth's strata accumulated bit by bit at the same speed as today's, the result of the calculation is "several tens of million years."

Apart from the above-mentioned evidence, there have been other extensive surveys of materials flowing from rivers to the ocean. Studies have been undertaken in relation to the ocean inflow of nickel, silicon, potassium, calcium, copper, mercury, tin, lead, zinc, cobalt, and many other materials. All of these studies have yielded the same results as those studies of salt density mentioned above.

It is also possible to estimate the maximum age of the earth by considering the "thickness of the earth's strata." On the assumption that the strata thickness gradually increased according to the speed at which sediment accumulates today on the ocean floor, we can estimate the time it took to reach its current thickness.

As previously explained, creationists reason that the earth's strata were formed largely in one hit, due to the occurrence of the Great Flood. However, assuming, as evolutionists do, that the earth's strata accumulated bit by bit at the same speed as today's, what kind of a result is yielded? The result is "several tens of million years."[12]

Apart from these methods, there are various other proofs available regarding the limit of the earth's age, but it all points to the same result. Therefore, Dr. Clark, a pioneer of synthetic chemical research into the earth's crust, commented in 1924,

"Chemistry, paleontology, and astronomy research agrees that the age of the earth is in the order of 50 to 150 million years."*[13]

Scientists at the dawn of the twentieth century considered the earth to be at most about this age.

5. Evolutionists Demand a "Long Time Period"

So, WHY and how did evolutionists come up with the figure of "4.5 billion years" with respect to the age of the earth?

In the mid-twentieth century, age-dating methods involving "radioactive isotopes" were invented. These methods included the carbon dating method mentioned earlier, as well as the potassium-argon method, uranium-lead method, rubidium-strontium method. Of these methods, the carbon dating method is the only one that directly dates the fossil itself, whereas the other methods estimate the age of surrounding rocks.

Radioactive isotope methods yielding the dates of rocks were enthusiastically embraced by evolutionists because, although their numerical values were very "discordant,"[14] they were very big numbers in the order of "several billion years." Evolutionists were extremely pleased with such results, because a "long period of time" is vital to their theory.

For evolutionists, the idea that "life and the universe evolved over a long time" is a kind of confession of religious faith, and they were keenly engaged in the hunt for apparent proof to support this. The evolutionist doctrine came first, followed by data supplied to lend weight to the doctrine. This is acknowledged by a famous Japanese evolutionist himself, who comments:

> "It is notable that evolutionist theory was not formulated in the order of gathering geological data first, and then reasoning that the history of the world is very long. In fact, it is quite the opposite…the hypothesis came first. That hypothesis was a presumptive intention, not sufficiently

evidenced by the data…. The data was interpreted
to fit the hypothesis."[15]

Thus, the idea that "evolution is a fact" came first, followed by evidence which was chosen and adopted in support of the idea. This is the reason why radioactive isotope
methods of dating, which yielded old dates in the order of
several billion years, were so enthusiastically welcomed
among evolutionists.

The Director of the Institute for Creation Research
(ICR) in the U.S.A., Dr. Henry M. Morris, in his book *What
is Creation Science?*, includes a graph of the results of various
estimates of the earth's age according to a variety of dating
methods. The results according to seventy different estimates are contained in the graph, and Dr. Morris comments
as follows:

> "All give ages far too young to accommodate the
> Evolution Model. All are based on the same
> types of calculations and assumptions used by
> evolutionists…"[16]

As this indicates, among the many methods for calcu-
lating the age of the earth, only those few methods such as
uranium, potassium, and rubidium methods yield very old
dates. Evolutionists have adopted these old dates, and dismissed the extensive alternative data yielding short time periods, saying there is "something improper in them."[17]

However, Dr. Morris has commented,

> "Nevertheless, all things considered, it seems that
> those ages on the low end of the spectrum are
> likely to be more accurate than those on the high
> end."[18]

And he gives several reasons for this proposition. The ages on the high end—the old end—are very likely to be highly inaccurate. Further, as will next be discussed, it is possible that an examination of the presumptions on which these radioactive isotope dating methods are based can yield a set of largely different results.

6. Nuclear Decay Rate Was Different

DATE MEASUREMENTS yielded by radioactive isotopes utilize the fact that radioactive chemical elements change to other elements as they emit radial rays over time. The period of time which it takes for 50 percent of atoms to change to other elements is called the "half-life."

For example, the half-life of potassium-40, uranium-238, rubidium-87 is said to be "1.3 billion years," "4.5 billion years," and "50 billion years" respectively. Thus, their half-lives are thought to be extremely long. It is not easy to estimate these long half-lives.

As a matter of fact, the estimation of half-life is based on a certain special assumption that the nuclear decay rate (or decay parameter) has not changed in the past, and has been constant throughout the ages.

This assumption presumes that, for example, the decay of 10 percent of all original atoms took a certain period of time, and the same period was required to decay 10 percent of those remaining atoms and so on, such that the decay continued at the same rate.

This assumption lies at the heart of the estimation of half-life. The half-life of uranium-238 is said to be 4.5 billion years, for example, but this does not mean that someone has measured this for over 4.5 billion years. Rather, this value is an assumption which has been calculated by magnifying several billion times the results of measurements obtained over several years.

In that process of magnifying, the assumption of constant rate of nuclear decay has been used. However, there is a possibility, as I will next discuss, that the nuclear decay rate was faster in the past.

The renowned American scientist Dr. Theodore W. Rybka in his treatise concerning nuclear decay, has commented on the possibility that the decay rate was faster in the past. Several matters suggested this is the case, including the implication arising from the relation between the speed of light and the nuclear decay rate.

It is known that, according to theory, the nuclear decay rate bears a certain relationship to the speed of light. Nuclear decay rate is "related to the energy of the ejected particle;" and "the energy is related to the velocity of light through the relativistic expression."[19]

The speed of light is currently said to be 300,000 kilometers (187,500 miles) per second in free space (but in water or in air it is much slower). However, there is currently no means of ascertaining whether this was also the speed in the past. Light is an electromagnetic wave, and its speed depends on the permittivity and (magnetic) permeability of space. So the speed of light could vary, depending on the conditions in cosmic space.

According to the Bible, there is a possibility that the conditions in cosmic space were once different from today's, during God's creation week; thus the speed of light was faster during that week. Genesis 1:16-18 records as follows:

> "God made two great lights—the greater light to govern the day and the lesser light to govern the night. He also made the stars. God set them in the expanse of the sky to give light on the earth, to govern the day and the night, and to separate light from darkness. And God saw that it was good."

This refers to the creation of the stars, and indicates that God made stars "to give light on the earth," and so they did. Namely, on the very day that God created the stars to shine in the night sky, the light of those stars could be seen on the earth.

On the very day that God created the stars, the light of those stars could be seen on the earth.

How far away from the earth are the stars (fixed stars) which we see in the night sky? With respect to stars outside our solar system, the closest star is the Alpha star in the Centaur constellation, which is 4.3 light-years away.

This means that it takes 4.3 years for the light to get to the earth from the star at the current light speed. Other stars are all further away. In other words, on the very day of creation of this star, which is 4.3 light-years away, and of other more distant stars, their light could be observed on the earth.

If one acknowledges this, then the possibility arises that the speed of light during the creation week was limitless or near limitless. If the speed of light was faster during the creation week, then we can say that the nuclear decay rate was also faster. And the half-lives of radioactive isotopes were very short. During the creation week, the nuclear decay rate of, for example, uranium 238 was very fast, and its half-life (said to be 4.5 billion years) was also very short.

So, on the day just after the six days of God's creation, the nuclear decay of radioactive isotopes, which is the basis for rock dating methods, was already far advanced. If one examined the age of rocks on that day by using today's nuclear decay rate, the result would indicate that the earth was already more than several billions of years old, although, in fact, its true age would be only six days.

This is all based on the assumption that the speed of light was faster during the creation week. Let me explain why this assumption does not conflict with my comment in a previous chapter that if light had different speed, then living things could not maintain life.

It was not until after the creation week that light maintained constant speed. During the creation week, the speed of light as well as the nuclear decay rate could have been different from today's because God was doing his work of creation. It was before God fixed the physical laws of the universe. During the creation week, the universe grew in perfect order under his perfect control and command.

So, if we admit that the speed of light was almost infinite during the creation week, it is very reasonable to think that the earth's age which is calculated according to today's nuclear decay rate is too old. The true age of the earth seems to be very young, less than 10,000 years.

Radioactive isotope dating methods are often regarded as extremely sound and beyond reproach, but actually there is a strong possibility that they are fundamentally flawed. In this regard, a famous evolutionist confesses in his book:

> "We always have the fear that the whole of our Age-Table according to radioactive isotope dating may be completely wrong from start to finish, due to some unexpected systematic errors."[*20]

Dr. Brian John, of Oxford University, also comments:

> "It is very likely that we will have to correct the dating of the past more substantively, facing up to some crucial problems."[*21]

Next, let us look at the other decisive evidence which reveals that the earth is very young.

7. The Earth Is Young

(1) Carbon-14 in the Atmosphere

ONE BODY of vital evidence indicating that the earth is young is the research into C-14 in the atmosphere.

C-14 is formed by the collision of high-energy neutrons flying from space with nitrogen-14 in the earth's atmosphere, and the amount of atmospheric C-14 thereby gradually increases. It is reasonable to suppose that the amount of neutrons flying from space over the ages has been constant. So the speed of increase in the amount of atmospheric C-14 has also been roughly the same since long ago.

On the other hand, as C-14 is radioactive material, it decays and decreases with the emission of radioactivity. The amount of decrease is proportionate to the original amount; the greater the original amount, the greater the decrease. Accordingly, the amount of atmospheric C-14 increases to a certain extent but once it reaches a specific level, it will not increase further. The amount of C-14 which is produced and the amount which decays and reduces obtain a balanced condition.

This is just like the phenomenon produced by pouring water into a bucket with a small hole in its bottom. As you pour the water in, the level of the water inside the bucket gradually rises but some water flows out due to the hole in the bottom. Then, once the water reaches a certain level, it will not increase any further. The inflowing water and outflowing water balance out and reach a stable, balanced condition.

The atmosphere is like a big bucket containing C-14. The amount of atmospheric C-14 increases gradually as neutrons collide with N-14 but also decreases as a result of radioactive decay.

So atmospheric C-14 gradually builds up to a certain level, but will not increase over that level once it reaches a balanced condition. Scientists know that this balanced condition is achieved in about 30,000 years.

Evolutionist claim that the earth's age is about 4.5 billion years, so the person who first came up with this figure said:

> "The amount of C-14 in the atmosphere must have reached a balanced condition in the distant past and thereafter maintained a constant level."

However, on examination, it has been discovered that such balanced condition has never been reached at all in the past. The result of an estimation of the amount of C-14 existing in the atmosphere reveals that only about 10,000 years have passed since the birth of the earth. Evolutionists are aware of this result and are perplexed by it. However, from the perspective of creationists, this result is very logical and understandable.

(2) Existence of Comets

SECONDLY, let us consider the important fact of the existence of comets in the solar system. Comets testify that the earth is young.

Comets are stars circling around the sun. It is thought that comets are formed mostly from ice. If they pass too close to the sun, they are blown to the surface by solar wind (radioactivity from the sun) and their trail can be seen from the earth.

The famous Haley's Comet has a large, long elliptical orbit and circles around the sun. It passes close by every 76 years so that the figure which drags its trail can be seen very clearly from the earth.

When a comet makes a trail in the sky, it gradually loses its own substance, such that with the passing of time, the comet becomes smaller and smaller.

Why do comets, that disappear after about 10,000 years, still exist today?

What period of time does it take for comets to get smaller and eventually disappear? It is estimated that this period is about 10,000 years for comets with a short orbital cycle, and a maximum 1,000,000 years for comets with a long orbital cycle.

Thus, if as evolutionists suggest, the age of the solar system is 5 to 6 billion years, then the fact that comets exist within the solar system even today is really a mysterious result. In fact, some evolutionists hypothesize that material from which comets originate exists in a place at the far reaches of the solar system, which cannot be observed from the earth. Without such a hypothesis, the fact that comets exist even today cannot be explained by evolutionists.

However, the original source of comets has never been observed and, theoretically speaking, it is difficult to understand how such matter exists.

So, the fact that comets exist today is regarded by creationists as evidence that the solar system is extremely young.

(3) Cosmic Dust

ANOTHER INDICATOR of vital evidence indicating that the earth is young is the research into "cosmic dust," which rains down to earth from space. These particles called "cosmic dust" are best thought of as extremely tiny meteorites, but as they fall to earth extremely slowly, they do not burn out in the atmosphere but accumulate bit by bit on the surface of the earth.

Scientists know the speed of cosmic dust accumulation approximately, but on the surface of the earth there are movements of the atmosphere and the oceans, which make it difficult to measure the amount of cosmic dust accumulation. However, on the moon, there is no atmosphere nor ocean, and no movement on its surface, so cosmic dust accumulates and remains as it is.

Evolutionists think that the moon is 4.5 billion years old—the same as the earth—and they used to think that the moon must have been covered with a thick accumulation of loose cosmic dust several tens of meters thick, which had been raining down on the moon for 4.5 billion years.

In fact, the chief astronaut of the *Apollo* spaceship, Mr. Neil Armstrong, the first man to walk on the moon, when asked in a TV interview about his initial thoughts on the moon landing, he said, "I was at first apprehensive that the ship might be buried in (cosmic) dust."*

He was taught the concept of an "old universe" and evolution, but actually, the ship and he were not buried in cosmic dust. The loose cosmic dust accumulated on the surface of the moon was only several millimeters thick.[22] It was surprisingly thin.

An American scientist Dr. Harold S. Slusher says:

The cosmic dust accumulated on the surface of the moon was surprisingly thin.

"The period of cosmic dust accumulation seems to be about 5-6 thousand years rather than several billion years."*[23]

The moon is very young; so is the earth.

Note: Some people argue about the existence of the regolith at least several meters thick beneath the loose dust on the lunar surface as a denying factor against the thought that the moon is young. This regolith consists of lunar rock debris produced by impacting meteorites mixed with dust, some of which is of meteoric origin.

As I mentioned in chapter 1, if we think that there was a time of collisions of asteroids during God's creation week, the regolith seems to be formed at the last stage of the collisions of asteroids. The fact that the regolith is a strongly compacted mixing layer of lunar materials with the incoming meteoritic influx shows that it was already formed in the primeval age, at the last stage of the collisions of asteroids on the moon.

On the other hand, we can think that the loose dust on the surface of the regolith has been accumulated in the quiet age after the stop of the collisions of asteroids. Concerning the age of the moon and the earth, we can think that the thin loose dust layer on the moon is still evidence that the moon and the earth are young.

(4) Decay of the Earth's Magnetic Field

NEXT, let us consider the important fact of the earth's magnetic field as an indicator that the earth is young. As is widely known, the earth is a huge magnet. Because of the earth's magnetic field, mountain climbers using a compass can find the right direction even in foggy conditions.

The earth's magnetic field has been measured every year since the first measurement in 1835. The result of these measurements shows that the earth's magnetic field is weakening. The energy of the magnetic field has decreased by about 14 percent since 1835. This is a rapid decline.

According to a publication of the U.S. government, if the weakening of earth's magnetic field continues at this rate, it will practically have disappeared in about 2000 years.[24]

Was the earth's magnetic field decaying before 1835, too?

It was. This is shown by archaeomagnetism, which is a study of magnetization of bricks, pottery, campfire stones, and other man-related objects studied by archaeologists. Iron oxides in those objects retain a record of the strength and direction of the earth's magnetic field at the time they last cooled to normal temperatures.

The data of old magnetized objects taken worldwide show that the intensity of the earth's magnetic field was about 40 percent greater in A.D. 1000 than it is today, and also was about 50 percent greater at the time of Christ.

However, before that, the data show that the earth's magnetic field fluctuated wildly up and down. This is also evidenced by paleomagnetism, which is the study of how magnetization locks into rocks at the time of their formation.

Paleomagnetic data show that while the geological strata were being laid down, the earth's magnetic field reversed its direction hundreds of times.

To explain this phenomenon, evolutionists have been working on "dynamo theories" for a long time, without great success. Furthermore, recent measurements of electric currents in the sea floor weigh heavily against the most popular class of dynamo theories.

However, a new theory (dynamic decay theory), which was recently proposed by the famous American scientist and creationist Dr. Russell Humphreys, explains these fluctuations of the earth's magnetic field very well. Dr. Humphreys' theory was applied to the prediction of the magnetic fields of Uranus and Neptune, and the prediction was proved to be right by the American outer space explorer *Voyager II*.

Although evolutionists estimated the magnetic field of Uranus to be none or very weak, the data which were sent from *Voyager II* when it passed near Uranus in 1986 supported Dr. Humphreys' theory—not evolutionist theory. Again, the data sent from *Voyager II* when it passed near Neptune in 1989 also matched his prediction.

Without going into a detailed explanation here, Dr. Humphreys' basic theory is that the earth's magnetic field was the strongest when the earth was just created, and then gradually decreased in strength. In about 2500 B.C., at the time of Noah, the Great Flood on the whole surface of the earth must have had some influence on the earth's inside, and some disturbance occurred in the flow of the inside fluid. As a result, the earth's magnetic field was influenced, producing rapid reversals and fluctuations.

The up-and-down fluctuations of the field at the earth's surface continued for more than 2,000 years afterwards. As a result, these fluctuations were recorded as paleomagnetic data of rocks in the strata which formed during and after the Great Flood. At or around the time of the birth of Christ, the earth's magnetic field settled to its natural condition, and from then on, it has been decreasing steadily at a constant rate until today.

Dr. Humphreys' theory explained very well the mechanism of the reversals and fluctuations of the earth's magnetic field. According to him, the total energy of the earth's magnetic field has always decreased since its birth to current day, and it especially decreased at the time of the reversals, numerous poles, and fluctuations caused by the Great Flood, because during that time the energy loss would have been faster than today's rate.

If we estimate the period dating from the present back to the past strongest limit of the earth's magnetic field, the result is a "maximum age of 8700 years."

Any estimation greater than this yields a measurement of the earth's magnetic field which is unrealistically strong. Therefore, the age of the earth could be at most 8700 years, but actually it is younger than that.

This result supports the Biblical assertion that the age of the earth is about 6000 years.[25]

(5) Lower and Upper Strata Formed in Same Period

NEXT, let us look at some important evidences which call into question the evolutionist assertion that the age of the earth is "several billion years," and which reveal the earth's age to be, in fact, less than 10,000 years.

The Grand Canyon in the U.S.A. is famous for its enormous mass of geological strata exposed over an extremely vast area. The Grand Canyon has one lava rock flow in the lower stratum, and the same kind of lava rock flow in the upper stratum. If the evolutionists are right, we might expect the lava rock at the bottom to be extremely old and that at the top to be very young.

A team of American creationist researchers investigated this matter, using the rubidium-strontium method which is employed by evolutionists. This method calculates age by measuring the ratio of rubidium to strontium within the lava rock. The research concluded that the ratio of rubidium to strontium in the lava rock flows in both the lower and upper strata is about the same. So, if we apply the evolutionist dating method, the date that the lava rock flows formed in both lower and upper strata was about "one billion years ago."

Whether or not this figure is "one billion years," we know for sure that the two lava rock flows occurred in the same period. The geological strata of both the lower and upper levels were formed around the same time.

This result is completely opposite to the claims of evolutionists, who assert that geological strata have built up slowly from bottom to top over many (several hundred million) years. Therefore, a conclusion that both lower and upper strata levels were formed at about the same time contradicts evolution theory.

In contrast, this result well suits the view of creationists, who reason that the geological strata lying above the layer referred to by evolutionists as Pre-Cambrian were formed largely in one hit at the time of Noah's Flood. Therefore, the conclusion that the lower and upper strata levels are about the same age is not surprising from a creationist perspective.

Creationists believe that Noah's Flood occurred about 4500 years ago. At that time, both the lower and upper strata levels were formed through accumulation of sediment by flooding. It is also thought that, at the time of the Great Flood, volcanic eruptions occurred here and there on the earth so lava rock flows were caught up in geological strata.

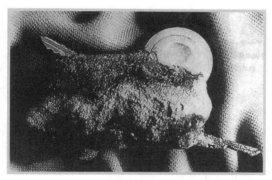

A key shut in a rock. (Museum of Creation and History of the Earth) Rock can be formed in several months.

Besides, if we consider that it is possible that the rubidium-strontium method contains a systematic error, it would yield dates which would be enormously different from the true dates. It can, then, be argued that the estimated result of about one billion years is, in reality, only about 4500 years, as held by creationists.

The same applies to other dating methods used by evolutionists such as the uranium-lead and potassium-argon methods. As these methods are all based on the same mistaken assumptions, they produce very significant and systematic errors. However, if a review of such assumptions is conducted, it is possible that these methods could also yield a result revealing the age of the earth to be about 10,000 years or less.

(6) Amount of Helium

WHAT ABOUT considerations related to the amount of helium in the atmosphere?

Helium is constantly produced by the decaying of radioactive substances, such as uranium, contained in rocks of the earth's crust, and that helium is then emitted into the earth's atmosphere.

One can thus guess the age of the atmosphere and the age of the earth by considering various factors including the amount of helium contained in the atmosphere, and the rate of emission of helium from rocks. In an essay by Dr. Duane T. Gish and Dr. Richard B. Bliss, the result of this estimation is described:

> "Estimating by the rate of addition of helium to the atmosphere from radioactive decay, the age of the earth appears to be about 10,000 years, even allowing for moderate helium escape."[26]

(7) Light of 15 Billion Years Ago?

NEXT, let us think about the age of the universe. I mentioned earlier that the speed of light during the six days of creation was unlimited or close to unlimited. This idea is essential to an understanding of the age of the universe.

Astronomists tell us that the most remote star lies about 15 billion light-years away. This means that at today's speed of light it would take about 15 billion years to reach that star. In this regard, an evolutionist has stated as follows,

> "The light which you can see from that star was emitted by it 15 billion years ago. In other words, you are looking at the form of a star from 15 billion years ago. From this, we can reason that the age of the universe is about 15 billion years."

However, if we accept that during the six days of creation of the universe the speed of light was much faster than today (as recorded in Genesis 1:17), then it is possible that the light from that star at the edge of the universe was emitted nowhere near 15 billion years ago. We can conclude that the light was emitted not in the distant past but relatively recently.

We do not see the form of the star from over 15 billion years ago. As the speed of light during the six days of creation was much faster than today, light from the vast space of the universe reached very close to the earth. That light can now be seen from the surface of the earth.

The true age of the universe is much younger than evolutionists would have us believe. It is not at all strange to consider the universe to be young, just like the earth, moon, and comets.

8. Can Life Be Generated in 4.5 Billion Years?

WE HAVE been repeatedly told for a long time that the earth is "several billion years old," and that the universe is "several tens of billion years old," that the conclusion that the earth and the universe are very young must sound a little strange to some people.

That is because we have in mind the preconception that these are very old. The assertion of evolution theory that "the world was born an inconceivably long time ago, life was generated over an extremely long period, and man evolved from there" has been taught to us time and again.

Is this really so? Let us assume for a time that the earth and the universe are both very old, as evolutionists say. If that were so, would there be enough time for life to form, evolve, and humankind to appear?

The renowned information scientist Marcel Golay estimated the probability of the simplest life forming naturally, throughout all of the ages of the entire universe.

Doubtful or uncertain factors involved in such estimation were, as far as possible, interpreted in a manner favorable to the evolutionist model, and he based the calculation on an assumption that the age of the universe is 3 trillion years (i.e. 200 times that estimated by evolutionists). Even on this basis, the possibility of matter combining successfully to naturally generate life was estimated to be one in 10^{280}.

10^{280} means 1 with 280 zeros following; in other words, one in 10^{280} is practically a zero chance.[27] To rephrase this result: it means that even if the age of the universe was assumed to be 3 trillion years multiplied by 10^{280}, there is little to no chance of life being naturally generated.

In fact, that possibility would be even smaller. Because, considering the "Law of Entropy" (the law that all changes are in the direction of increasing entropy, of increasing disorder,

If the age of the earth is 4.5 billion years, or even 3 trillion years multiplied by 10^{280}, the chance of life being generated naturally is zero.

of increasing randomness, of running down), the older the universe is, the more impossible it is that things evolve to high order.

So, if the age of the earth is 4.5 billion years, or even 3 trillion years multiplied by 10^{280}, then the chance of life being generated naturally is zero. This reveals that the idea "if the world's history is long enough, then life must have come about during that time" is fundamentally incorrect.

We do not have to insist on such a long period of time. Instead of thinking that the earth and life on it appeared over a long period, it stands to reason to suppose that, as the Bible explains, earth and life were created relatively recently.

There is a large body of evidence revealing that the earth is young. The appearance of life has also been recent, since it was created soon after the earth's formation, and appeared "according to their kinds" (Genesis 1:11).

9. No Such Age As So-Called Prehistory

ANTHROPOLOGY based on evolutionist doctrine generally divides the history of human kind into "historical ages" and "prehistorical ages."

"Historical ages" refer to ages which are known to us by virtue of written records, and commence, on the whole, from the age when "urban culture" or civilization was first in evidence.

The oldest use of the written word is currently thought to be about 5000 years ago. As the oldest civilization known today is that of Mesopotamia, which is said to have commenced about 6000 years ago, the ages of history can thus be regarded as commencing from about 6000 years ago.

According to evolutionist paleontology, before such time there were "prehistorical ages" or ages "before the commencement of history." However, as we have already seen, the earth and man are much younger than evolutionists think, and a long period of time such as several billion years has not passed since they came into being.

There has, in fact, been no long time period during which human beings have "evolved" from lower life-forms. So human beings have not evolved from inferior beings to their current form.

Homo sapiens appeared together with other animals after they were originally created several thousand years ago—some 6000 years ago. This means that at about the same time as the birth of man, the world entered its age of history. There was no prehistorical period existing before that time.

According to the Bible, from the time man was created, there was a certain degree of civilization, culture, and written word in existence, and this means it was already the age of history. The Bible tells that a primitive form of word or letter was used in the case of Adam's son Cain, for example, when he was banished after committing murder, and God "put a mark on Cain" (Genesis 4:15). Whatever form this mark took, there can be no doubt that it represents the beginning of written words.

Mankind entered "the age of history" from the start of its existence.

That the use of written words occurred very early on is clear, since from Adam's time history has been recorded in detail, and later collected to form the Bible.

Further, various forms of civilization were in existence from the start. After the Fall of Man, God fashioned "garments of skin" for Adam and Eve, and from then the custom of wearing clothes commenced.

Since the Bible records that "Cain worked the soil" (Genesis 4:2), agriculture was certainly practiced, and probably there were also stone tools to cultivate the land, which man could already make by himself.

When Adam and Eve became aware of their nakedness, they "sewed fig leaves together and made coverings for themselves." (Genesis 3:7) Man already had at that time skills for processing things to make them more useful, and they probably already knew how to make certain tools.

Furthermore, as the Bible records, Adam's second son, Abel, became a "keeper of flocks," and after him Jabal also raised livestock, so we know that at least from as early as Abel's time, stock farming was already in existence. (Genesis 4:2, 20)

Urban civilization was also established from an early period. After Cain was banished, Adam and Eve gave birth to sons and daughters (Genesis 5:4). Cain married one of the daughters and "built a city" (Genesis 4:17).

About 3500 B.C., Cain's descendant Jubal became the founder of musical culture of the harp and flute (Genesis 4:21), and his brother Tubal-Cain became the founder of bronze and iron tools (Genesis 4:22).

Thus, according to the Bible, mankind possessed, just soon after its birth, various kinds of civilized cultural skills, and was an urban dweller from early on. In other words, man entered "the age of history" from the start of his existence.

It should also be noted that what is generally known of the content of historical ages accords very well with the record of history in the Bible. Various archaeological facts not only support the historical ages recorded in the Bible, but also are very useful to clarify many of their details.

10. Interpretation of Genesis, Chapter 1, Verses 1 and 2

FINALLY, let us look at some interpretations of the Bible concerning the creation week recorded in Genesis chapter 1.

Scientists who support the theory of evolution estimate that the age of the universe is approximately 15 billion years (or 20 billion years) according to the big bang theory. On the other hand, the Bible states that the universe was created in six days about 6000 years ago. The timescale of these two approaches is thus completely different.

In order to resolve this timescale variance, people have sought to interpret the Bible in various ways, and among such interpretations, the two main ones are as follows:

(1) Gap Theory

THIS THEORY maintains that, between verses 1 and 2 of Genesis chapter 1, there was an intermission (gap) of several billion years. In other words, between the scripture verses:

"In the beginning God created the heavens and the earth."

and

"Now the earth was formless and empty, darkness was over the surface of the deep…"

it is thought that there was a gap of several billion years. This theory acknowledges a very long period of time, but the word "day" referred to in Genesis chapter 1 is thought to mean actually about twenty-four hours (the time of one rotation of the earth).

(2) Day-Age Theory

THIS THEORY propounds that the each "day" referred to in Genesis chapter 1 does not mean the time of one rotation of the earth (about twenty-four hours), but a much longer period in the order of billions of years.

(3) Problems Relating to the Gap Theory and Day-Age Theory

ARE THESE interpretations of the Bible at all viable?

Let us first look at the gap theory. This proposes that the universe was created at Genesis 1:1, and after that, a lapse of time of billions of years passed, and at verse 2 onward, God created the sky, sea, land, plants, animals, and human beings, etc…

In the case of this theory, the "day" referred to in verse 2 and following means literally about twenty-four hours, or one night and day. In other words, the separation of "water above the expanse," the air and the sea on the second day, and the formation of the continents on the third day, and all events on and following the fourth day, are thought to have occurred within about twenty-four hour literal days.

In order to reason that such large-scale changes to the earth occurred within respective twenty-four hour periods, it is necessary to embrace a belief in the almighty creative power of God.

If we believe that God brought about these changes to the earth within six days, the question arises as to why it is necessary to impose a gap in time of "several billion years" between verses 1 and 2 of Genesis, to achieve a forced consensus with today's theory of evolution?

The gap theory is highly fallible, mixing elements of both evolutionist and creationist ideas. It is clearly unworkable from a Biblical perspective, and also from the point of view of science, it is a half-measure and gives rise to controversy.

So what about the day-age theory mentioned above? Is it possible to regard each "day" of creation of the universe as referring to a much longer period such as several billion years?

In fact, this interpretation also gives rise to many problems. The Bible states that plants such as flowers, trees, and fruits were created on the third day of creation. Now we all know that insects are essential to the pollination of plants, which is achieved by insects sucking nectar from flowers and carrying pollen to plant pistils.

Insects are vital especially to the pollination of plants such as cucumbers, mulberries, or chestnut trees, which have distinctly separate staminate (male) flowers and pistillate (female) flowers. They cannot be pollinated except with the aid of insects. However, the Bible records that insects were not created until the fifth day.

Thus, a major difficulty arises with respect to this day-age theory: how did plant species continue to be pollinated in the absence of insects, which would not have been created until several billion years later?

Furthermore, this theory has a Biblical problem. In Exodus 20:10,11, the Bible states,

"The seventh day is a Sabbath to the Lord your God…. For in six days the Lord made the heavens and the earth, the sea and all that is in them, but he rested on the seventh day".

If each "day" in the creation week meant one age of billions of years, we would have to work during the ages of billions of years multiplied by six, and after that, we could rest at last. Thus, unless the "day" means actually a day, the Bible verses have no meaning.

The people who assert the "day" to be one age sometimes refer to the verse: "With the Lord one day is like a thousand years, and a thousand years like one day" (II Peter 3:8). But this Bible verse means only that there is no big difference, from the standpoint of the eternal living God, between a day and a thousand years. This verse does not mean that each "day" of the creation week is a very long period of time.

Clearly the day-age theory oversteps the bounds of reason. It gives rise to problems in view of the Bible, and also in view of the known scientific facts.

So, there are problems inherent in both the gap theory and the day-age theory. They are problematical both from a Biblical and a scientific point of view.

11. Third Interpretation

Next, let us look at a third interpretation of creation. This theory involves a literal interpretation of the Bible.

According to this third interpretation, there is no gap of several billion years between Genesis 1:1 and 1:2. Further, the "days" of creation are taken to mean literally the time of one rotation of the earth—i.e., one night and day, or about twenty-four hours.

As many theologians and Jewish rabbis point out, the original Hebrew scripture of Genesis 1:1 and 1:2 can also be translated, "When God began to create the heavens and earth, the earth was [as yet] formless and empty."

The expression, "In the beginning, God created the heavens and the earth," is generally so famous that most translations conform to this wording. But the original Hebrew can also be translated as "When God began to create…"

"In the beginning, God created…"—these famous words of scripture leave a vivid impression in our hearts. However, the translation, "When God began to create the heavens and the earth…" seems to better express the content of Genesis chapter 1.

The former and the latter translations both record that God did create the heavens and earth (from nothingness). However, in the latter translation, verses 1 and 2 of Genesis chapter 1 are connected as one passage. In other words, there is no "gap" of several billion years between Genesis 1:1 and 1:2. Thus the passage reads:

"In the beginning, on the first day of God's commencement of creation of the heavens and the earth, the earth was void and without form."

Thus, if we carefully study the original Hebrew, we find that the description in the Bible begins with the time when God first began to create the universe, when the earth was "formless and empty."

At the beginning of the first day of creation, the universe was drawn out of nothingness and explosively brought to existence, and various kinds of matter were created therein, including the primitive earth in a chaotic form. That is what is meant by, "When God began to create the heavens and the earth, the earth was formless and empty." So it was a very rapid progression from the birth of the universe to the formation of the primitive earth. The primitive earth was shaped largely by the end of the first half of the first day.

In other words, according to the third interpretation, it took only half a day from the birth of the universe until the formation of the primitive earth.

There appears to be two possible approaches to the method by which the universe came to be born.

The first is that the universe was created from the very start as a wide expanse, and emerged silently. As this approach regards the universe as having a wide expanse from the very beginning, it is easy to understand how the basic structure of the universe could have been formed within half a day of creation.

The second idea is that the universe started out from one point and developed explosively into a wide expanse.

This idea is akin to the big bang theory. However, according to the big bang theory, it took ten billion years or more for the basic structure of the universe to be established, so the big bang theory does not strictly accord with this "third interpretation" estimate of "half a day."

However, ignoring this time period difference, the big bang theory idea that "the universe started from a single point and came into existence explosively" seems to be able to correspond with the Biblical description, "he (God) who created the heavens and stretched them out…" (Isaiah 42:5)

The Bible indicates that within the first half of Day One of creation, the universe came into existence explosively, and was stretched out.

I use the word "explosion," in a figurative sense, not like an explosion of dynamite occurring inside space. However, explosive birth of the universe refers to the sudden expansion of the universe as a whole—in a continuum of space, time, and substance, not the "explosion inside something." I refer to the sudden, dramatic expansion of space itself, and the sudden appearance of the material world itself. Totally different from a dynamite explosion, it is the kind of explosion which we have difficulty in imagining.

Ordinary explosions like that of dynamite have destructive effects, completely unlike the "explosive birth of the universe." The universe was not created "from out of an explosion" but rather, born "explosively."

The idea that space, time, and matter appeared explosively out of nothingness, unfolded into being and took shape does not contradict the Biblical account. So then, how should we regard the time period of billions of years which the big bang theory proposes?

The current big bang theory remains incomplete, and is still the subject of sharp controversy among scientists. The theory still gives rise to many questions, and leaves ground for widespread change in the future. There are bound to be new discoveries in the field of universe theories which will bring new developments.

The big bang theory maintains that the age of space is 15 billion years, assuming that rules of physics and chemistry apply constantly during the period from the first day of the birth of the universe to this date. In particular, this figure depends on the assumption that the speed of light has always been 300,000 kilometers (187,500 miles) per second.

As we discussed previously, it is conceivable that the speed of light, during the six-day period of the creation of the universe, was practically infinite. So, in other words, even in acknowledging the big bang, we do not have to accept the universe as being so incredibly ancient as 15 billion years.

The universe simply appears old—to those who think it is old.

To understand this idea, it is helpful to recall the verses of the Bible regarding the creation of Adam. Adam was created on the sixth day of creation. On that day, he appeared in the shape of a grown-up; he probably looked to be over twenty years old. But he was actually less than twenty-four hours old.

So it is with the age of the universe. The universe appeared after the six-day period of creation, and at that time it was only six days old. But as the universe was in completed form, it looked like as if it had already existed for a long time.

Whichever way we think that the universe was born—as a wide expanse, or that it came into existence explosively, the universe did come into existence from nothingness by God and was formed during the six-day period of creation.

This is the third interpretation with respect to the birth of the universe.

12. Theory in Accordance with the Bible Is the Correct Choice

ACCORDING TO the Bible, when the earth first came into being in a chaotic form on the first day of creation, it was already covered by "waters" (Genesis 1:2). This expression seems to refer to the thick water vapor atmosphere that covered the primitive earth.

In the latter half of the first day of creation something like the pre-sun had begun to exist, and radiated light at God's command, "Let there be light"(Genesis 1:3), , and lit up the earth. At that time, the sun was in a preliminary stage, before the commencement of nuclear fusion, but it gave light to the earth night and day.

On the second day, the "waters" (water vapor atmosphere) were separated into three: "water above the expanse" (water vapor canopy above the atmosphere, Genesis 1:7), the sky (atmosphere) and the ocean.

On the third day, the continents were created on the surface of the earth, and land and sea were separated. Plants were also created on the earth's surface on the same day.

Day Four saw the creation of the sun, moon and stars. The sun and fixed stars became the heavenly bodies which emitted a stable supply of light through nuclear fusion.

On the fifth day, all kinds of aquatic animals, birds, etc. were created; and on the sixth day, land animals, including human beings, were created.

Thus, the "days" should be taken literally, meaning about twenty-four hours—the time for one rotation of the earth. If it is God who created the entire universe, then there is no need whatsoever to argue that an exceedingly long period of time (in the order of billions of years) was required for creation.

Man is the highest creation.

At least from a Biblical perspective, this interpretation does not create any problems. In fact, many creationists with profound knowledge of science have accepted this interpretation as a very persuasive argument. In Genesis 2:2, the Bible records:

> "...on the seventh day (of creation) God rested from all his work."

It was on Day Seven that God rested. In other words, up to the preceding day, God had been actively involved in the progression of the universe. Therefore, during the first six days of God's creation, the laws of physics and chemistry in the universe must not have been as they are today.

God participated in the universe during the six days in a very special way. God created the universe; a period of six days must have been more than enough time for him.

SUMMARY

✦

THE UNIVERSE was called into being by a "God…who calls things that are not as though they were…" (Romans 4:17).

It is conceivable that, beginning with the "first dust of the world" (Proverbs 8:26 NASB), innumerable particles of dust came into existence in space, and formed the earth and other stars. There is a theory that the dust first formed asteroids, and then the earth was born through a process of their collision and merging.

The former stage of the sun, or "pre-sun," was also born at the heart of the solar system, and later became the sun we know today, supplying a stable light source, through nuclear fusion.

The earth, at the time of its birth, was covered by a vast "water vapor atmosphere" made up mostly of water vapor. But in a very short period of time in comparison to the history of the earth, this separated into "water above the expanse" (water vapor canopy), "the sky" (atmosphere), and "water under the expanse" (ocean) (Genesis 1:7).

At first the ocean covered all the earth's surface, which had few high and low spots, but then a landmass appeared out of the ocean, such that land and sea became divided. The land at that time was one whole mass.

Thereafter, plants created on the earth emitted oxygen through a process of photosynthesis, and increased the amount of oxygen within the atmosphere. Plants, being composed of various organic substances, were also very suitable as a source of nourishment for animals and human beings.

Because of the water vapor canopy above the atmosphere of the earth before the Great Flood, the entire surface of the earth was very temperate, as if in a greenhouse, regardless of whether the latitude was high or low.

There were no deserts or permanent ice fields, and the earth was covered in lush vegetation, sustaining enormous creatures, including the dinosaurs.

However, in the days of Noah, the water vapor canopy became heavy rain, which poured on the earth for "40 days and 40 nights." The water washed all over the earth. (Genesis 7:4, 17)

But even after the downpour stopped, the sea level continued to rise and "flooded the earth for 150 days" (Genesis 7:24). This was mostly caused by the undulation changes on the earth's surface. Great changes occurred on the cooled down surface, and "the mountains rose; the valleys sank down." (Psalm 104:8 NASB)

These changes began almost certainly in the ocean region first, pushing up the ocean bed to make submarine mountains, which pushed up the sea level and caused the flood waters to swell even further.

However, after that, "the water receded steadily from the earth"(Genesis 8:3). That is because mountains rose, and valleys sank down in each area of the world. The earth's surface became sharply undulated. Water accumulated in lower regions, and the areas above sea level became land.

The high mountains we see on the earth, and submarine mountains, as well as the great ocean depths were formed by the catastrophic crustal changes brought about by the Great Flood. These changes also caused the once uniform landmass of the earth to separate into its current form.

Owing to the Great Flood, many plants and animals became extinct. This is evidenced by the many fossils of living creatures such as frozen mammoths, and others, caught in a final death struggle in the strata of the earth.

The formation of geological strata is much more lucidly explained by the idea of the Great Flood, rather than the theory of evolution. While evolution theory gives rise to many contradictions and unclear points with respect to strata and fossils therein, the concept of the Great Flood generates no such contradictions.

Generally speaking, when the Great Flood began, creatures dwelling in the ocean floor were caught in the lowest stratum, and above them were fish and other amphibious species which could swim. Next came the land dwelling creatures: They were caught in higher strata because they lived in much higher places than marine life, and had much better migratory capacity.

As human beings had the most advanced migratory capacity, as well as the knowledge of how to escape from the water, their fossils are generally found in the highest strata.

The strata of the earth formed very swiftly, due to the Great Flood, and various fossils formed within the accumulated strata. Without this catastrophic process, fossils could never have been formed.

Following the Great Flood, the aspect of the earth's surface changed completely. The climate changed, and polar regions became closed off by ice. The topographical shape was reformed, and the ecological circumstances of living creatures were also transformed.

After disappearance of the water vapor canopy above, the earth became more exposed to cosmic rays and ultraviolet rays, such that the life expectancy of human beings was shortened.

Evolutionists estimate the age of the earth to be about 4.5 billion years, and the age of man to be about 2 to 3 million years, but there is a large body of reliable evidence which indicates that the age of both earth and mankind is far younger.

Evolutionists require a "long time period." But even assuming that the earth's age is 4.5 billion years or more, the probability of life being generated naturally on the earth is substancially zero.

It is far more reasonable to think that, as the Bible records, the earth and all that lives upon it, including human beings, appeared by being created in the relatively recent past.

Epilogue

✦

IN ORDER to elaborate more precisely on the matters touched upon in this book, it is necessary to think about problems related to the birth of life, and the question of how to view the theory of evolution of species. For a treatment of these issues, I wrote the sequel to this book titled *Science Comes Closer To The Bible: Part 2—Biology, Archaeology and Paleontology.* (The Japanese and Korean versions are already published.)

We have been told at school that humankind has come from the process of evolution, but today the "evidence" of such evolution is falling apart, to the point that it cannot really be regarded as evidence of evolution at all. The sequel to this book provides further commentary on this matter.

Many scientists are recognizing the inherent errors in evolutionist theory, and are abandoning it. In fact, there now exists in America a group of several thousand scientists and intellectuals who have abandoned evolution theory in favor of creationism.

Similar groups have been established in Japan, Australia, Canada, Russia, England, New Zealand, Korea and other countries, and they are very active.

Many facts which have been clearly established as a result of scientific research actually favor creation theory rather than evolution theory. The idea that man was especially created in the manner recorded in the Bible, rather than emerging as a result of evolution, can more easily explain a variety of known scientific facts.

Finally I wish to express my heartfelt gratitude, first to the Japanese readers of *Remnant* magazine who encouraged me to write this book, and also to Doctor of Medicine, Masami Usami, who has been carrying on scientific research of creationism for many years, to his son Minoru Usami, to the president of EastWest United Corporation and translator Mr. Iwao Miyamoto, to the translators Ms. Miriam Doi, Mr. Ken Yamada, Rev. Carlton Elkins, to Mr. Steve Laube of ACW Press, and to Mr. Fred Renich of Pine Hill Graphics for their cooperation.

I think the content of this book still has a long way to go, but I pray that it will assist in the spread of scientific creationism.

Arimasa Kubo

References

Chapter 1

1. Kitano, Yasushi, 1983. Mize To Chikyu No Rekishi, NHK Books, Japan, p.214.
2. Ijiri, Syouji and Minato, Masao, 1983. Chikyu No Rekishi, Iwanami-shinsyo, Japan, p.6.
3. Takeuchi, Hitoshi and Ueda, Masaya, 1984. Chikyu No Kagaku, NHK Books, Japan, p.209.
4. Matsui, Takafumi, 1987. Chikyu Uchu Soshite Ningen, Tokuma Syoten, Japan, pp.117-138.
5. Ojima, Minoru, 1981. Chikyushi, Iwanami-shinsyo, Japan, p.63.
6. Sagan, Carl, 1980. Cosmos, Oubunsya, Japan, III p.70.
7. Ojima, Ref. 5, p.150.
8. Ojima, Ref. 5, p.150.
9. Ojima, Ref. 5, p.155.
10. Ojima, Ref. 5, p.156.
11. Matsui, Ref. 4, p.191.
12. Gish, Duane T., Have You Been Brainwashed?, New Life League Pamphlet.
13. Ijiri and Minato, Ref. 2, p.6.
14. Ijiri and Minato, Ref. 2, p.25.
15. Takeuchi, Hitoshi and Miyashiro, Akiho, 1965. Chikyu No Rekishi, NHK Books, Japan, p.163.
16. Kitano, Ref. 1, p.214.
17. Kitano, Ref. 1, p.200.

Chapter 2

1. Newton, Kyouikusya, Japan, April 1986, p.42.
2. Scientific American, May 1984, p.128.
3. Morris, Henry M., 1976. The Genesis Record, Baker Book House Co. Michigan, p.52.
4. Obi, Shinya, 1980. Taiyoukei No Kagaku, NHK Books, Japan, p.23.
5. Obi, Ref. 4, p.23.
6. Butterfield and Bragg. Kindai Kagaku No Ayumi, Iwanami-shinsyo, Japan, p.29.

7. Hatanaka, Takeo, 1985. Uchu To Hoshi, Iwanami-shinsyo, Japan, p.45.
8. Morris, Ref. 3, p.60.
9. Tachibana, Takashi, 1985. Uchu Karano Kikan, Chukoh Bunko, Japan, p.265.
10. Saishin Uchu-ron, 1988. Gakken Moo Science Series II, Japan, p.44.
11. Saishin Uchu-ron, Ref. 10, p.46.

Chapter 3

1. Heinze, Thomas, 1975. Souzouka Shinkaka, Seisyo Tosyo Kankoukai, Japan, p.170.
2. Halley, Henry H., 1980. Seisyo Handbook, Seisyo Tosyo Kankoukai, Japan, p.75.
3. Halley, Ref. 2, p.75.
4. Morris, Henry M., 1976. The Genesis Record, Baker Book House Co., p.59
5. Tsukioka, Seiko. Anatano Sosenwa, Seisyo Tsushin kyoukai Tract, Japan, p.5.
6. Takeuchi, Hitoshi and Ueda, Masaya, 1984. Chikyu No Kagaku, NHK Books, Japan, p.35.
7. Seibutsu-kai No Shinpo, 1941, Japan, pp.12-13.
8. Mahanaimu, Seisyo To Kagaku No Kai, Japan, No.13, p.2.
9. Matsui, Takafumi, 1987. Chikyu Uchu Soshite Ningen, Tokuma Syoten, Japan, p.183.
10. Matsui, Ref. 9, p.191.
11. Allaby, Michael and Loveloch, James, 1986. Kyouryu Wa Naze Zetsumetsu Shitaka, Kodansya Blue Backs, Japan, p.10.
12. Allaby and Lovelock, Ref.11, chapter 5.
13. Kyoryu No Chi Wa Atatakakatta, 1987. Nikkei Science Sha, Japan, p.13.
14. Allaby and Lovelock, Ref.11, p.93.
15. ICR, 1971, California, p.52.
16. Jan. 16 1960, pp.39, 82-83.
17. Impact, ICR, California, No.168 p.3.
18. Impact, Seisyo To Kagaku No Kai, Japan, No.84 pp.2-3.
19. Impact, Ref. 18. No.28 p.5.
20. Rhodes, F.H.T., Zim, H.S. and Shaffer P.R., 1962. Fossils, Golden Press, New York, p.10.
21. Impact, Ref. 17, No.6 p.3.
22. Mahanaimu, Ref. 8, No.99 p.1.
23. Heinze, Ref. 1, p.167.
24. Stanfields, 1977. Shinka No Kagaku, Makumiran Syuppan, Japan, p.76.
25. Ijiri, Syouji and Minato, Masao, 1974. Chikyu No Rekishi, Iwanami-sin-syo, Japan, pp.61-62.
26. Impact, Ref. 17, No.32 p.3.
27. Impact, Ref. 18, No.14 p.3.
28. Halley, Ref. 2, p.74.
29. Lapple, Alfred, 1966. Seisyo No Sekai, Yamamoto Shoten, Japan, p.55.

Chapter 4

1. Sagan, Carl, 1980. Cosmos, Oubunsha, Japan, III p.70.
2. Sagan, Ref. 1, p.94.
3. Heinze, Thomas F., 1975. Souzouka Shinkaka, Seisyo Tosyo Kankoh Kai, Japan, p.62.
4. Mahanaimu, Seisyo To Kagaku No Kai, Japan, No.54 p.8.
5. Mahanaimu, Ref. 4, No.9 p.3.
6. Mahanaimu, Ref. 4, No.9 p.3.
7. Ojima, Minoru, 1981. Chikyu-shi, Iwanami-sinsyo, Japan, p.120.
8. Mahanaimu, Ref. 4, No.9 p.4.
9. Mahanaimu, Ref. 4, No.9 p.4.
10. Baker, Silvia, 1983. Sinkaron No Souten, Seisyo To Kagaku No Kai, Japan, p.93.
11. Takeuchi, Hitoshi and Miyashiro, Akiho, 1983. Chikyu No Rekishi, NHK Books, Japan, p.28.
12. Takeuchi and Miyashiro Ref. 11, p.28.
13. Takeuchi and Miyashiro Ref. 11, p.38.
14. Takeuchi and Miyashiro Ref. 11, p.38.
15. Takeuchi and Miyashiro Ref. 11, p.26.
16. Morris, Henry M. and Parker Gary E., 1982. What is CREATION SCIENCE?, Master Books, California, p.285.
17. Takeuchi and Miyashiro, Ref. 11, p.42.
18. Morris and Parker, Ref. 16, p.286
19. Impact, ICR, California, No.106 p.2.
20. Wilson, Colin, 1980. Jikan No Hakken, Mikasa Syobo, Japan, p.200.
21. Wilson, Ref. 20, p.200.
22. Impact, Seisyo To Kagaku No Kai, Japan, No.29 p.3.
23. Impact, Ref. 22, No.29 p.3.
24. Impact, Ref. 22, No.37 p.4.
25. Impact, Ref. 19, No.242.
26. Impact, Ref. 19, No.95 p.6.
27. Morris and Parker, Ref. 16, p.65.

Science Comes Closer to the Bible
Order Form

Please send *Science Comes Closer to the Bible* **to:**

Name: _____

Address: _____

City: _____ State: _____

Zip: _____

Telephone: (_____) _____

Book Price: $12.99

Shipping: $3.00 for the first book and $1.00 for each additional book to cover shipping and handling within US, Canada, and Mexico. International orders add $6.00 for the first book and $2.00 for each additional book.

Order from:
ACW Press
5501 N. 7th. Ave. #502
Phoenix, AZ 85013

(800) 931-BOOK

or
Amazon
(http://www.amazon.com/)

Barnes and Noble
(http://www.bn.com/)

Spring Arbor / Ingram Distributors
(http://www.springarbor.com/)
(http://www.ingram.com/)

or

contact your local bookstore

Science Comes Closer to the Bible
English, Japanese, Korean and Chinese Versions
Information: http://www5.ocn.ne.jp/~magi9/sciencec.htm

Contact address for author:
Arimasa Kubo
2260-13 Kodama, Kodama-machi
Kodama-gun, Saitama 367-0212
JAPAN

Phone or fax: [81] (495) 72-6203
E-mail: remnant@mte.biglobe.ne.jp